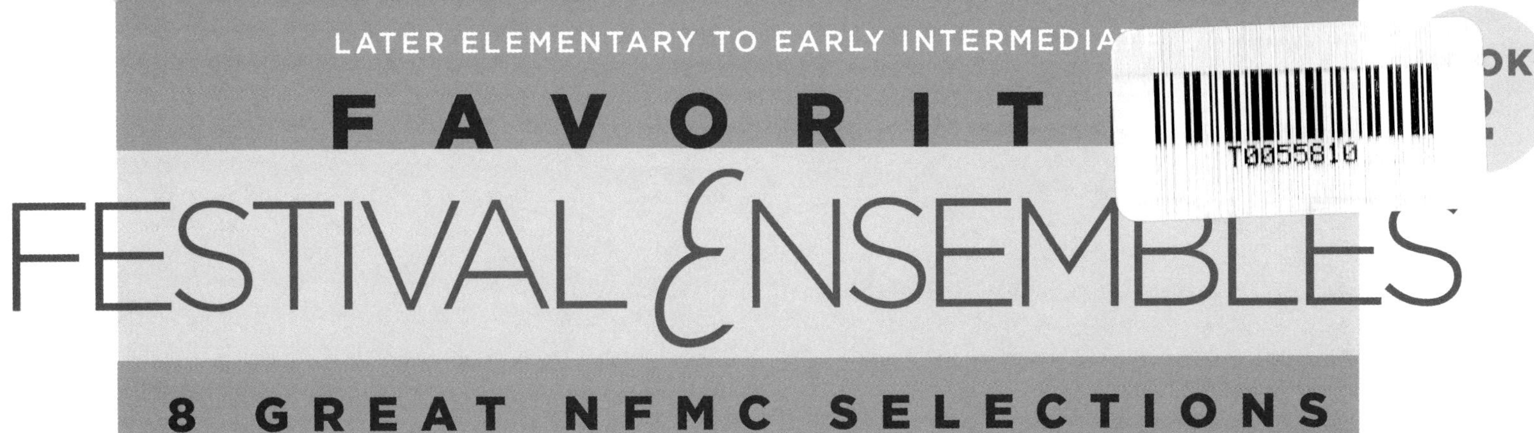

8 GREAT NFMC SELECTIONS

The **National Federation of Music Clubs (NFMC)** is a non-profit philanthropic music organization whose goal is to promote American music, performers, and composers through quality music education and supporting the highest standards of musical creativity and performance.

ISBN 978-1-4803-4198-2

Exclusively Distributed By

HAL•LEONARD®
CORPORATION
7777 W. BLUEMOUND RD. P.O. BOX 13819
MILWAUKEE, WISCONSIN 53213

CONTENTS

PERFORMANCE NOTES FROM THE **COMPOSERS**

EDITOR'S NOTE: Special thanks to Glenda Austin for providing notes on the Gillock pieces.

THE CHASE / Carolyn Miller and David Engle

NFMC 1995-1997

This duet requires crisp staccato and attention to phrasing. The Primo has the melody at the beginning, with additional voices added to both parts in measure 11. At measure 19, the chase begins! Practice the Primo part at measure 29, envisioning it as a lively chase between the hands. Bring out the harmonic surprises in the Secondo in measures 43-48. The ending for both parts should be clean, crisp and *forte*.

PINWHEELS / Katherine Beard

NFMC 1998-2000

A trio for 3 at one piano, or 6 at two pianos! Each student should know their own part perfectly before playing with the others. The players must count out loud until all three parts can be played securely together.

Playing with the metronome will be a great help in working up speed, and in assuring that the players will feel a steady beat after the metronome goes off. Fingering must be precisely observed. Each part is fingered to fit a small hand and to permit good phrasing and smooth playing of scale passages. For the best musical effect, watch the expression marks carefully.

KIBBUTZ CAPERS / David Karp

NFMC 1995-1997

The *kibbutz* (Hebrew word for "communal settlement") is a unique rural community which began in Israel. People living in a *kibbutz* work together and often dance together. This duet reflects the *kibbutzim* dancing. Many of the early Hebrew dances were in the minor mode. Check those dynamic indications; and remember, the accompaniment is generally played softer than the melody. Have fun as you bring out the melodies, and listen for a good balance between the parts.

PETITE SPANISH DANCE / Carolyn Miller

NFMC 2001-2003

This duet was always a favorite in my piano classes. It's easy to put together once you learn the basic rhythm patterns. The introduction should be played *forte* with lots of energy in both parts. Both players should be aware of which part has the melody and adjust their volume accordingly. I hope you enjoy the harmonies in measures 36-38.

By the way, this piece features a tango rhythm, but my students always shout "cha, cha, cha" at the end. Have fun!

ORIENTAL BAZAAR / William Gillock

NFMC 1995-1997

"Oriental Bazaar" is a piece that charmingly intertwines three separate parts to produce an effective, full sound. Part 3 plays a rhythmic and melodic *ostinato* throughout, while Parts 1 and 2 are responsible for the lyrical, melodic line in duet intervals of 4ths and 5ths.

On a personal note, this piece is special because it was dedicated to my sister Gloria and me. After completing the piece, Mr. Gillock came to Joplin and we met at my sister's home to "test" the hand positions of each part. Of course, it worked quite well; there were few, if any, changes. Afterwards, we went to Red Lobster for a special luncheon. We talked for hours, and a good time was had by all.

POLKA / David Karp

NFMC 1991-1994

The polka is a lively dance found in the United States. The most famous is the North American "Polish-style polka," with roots in Chicago. The time signatures are in *alla breve* (cut-time) and the melodies are enhanced with a combination of *legato* and staccato touches. Observing the articulations will make the music sound more lively and joyous. This polka begins in C Major and modulates to G Major (measure 19) before returning to C Major. End with a rousing *glissando*!

WESTERN BOLERO / David Karp

NFMC 1991-1994

The *bolero* has been popular for over a century and had its origins in Spain and Cuba. The Cuban *bolero* traveled to Mexico and the rest of Latin America where it became part of their repertories. The accompaniment in the Secondo is very typical of *bolero* rhythm—syncopation and off-beat accents abound in both melody and accompaniment. The quarter-note triplet in the penultimate measure may be achieved by counting in two (*alla breve*); start a few measures before the end.

TREPAK / Tchaikovsky, arr. William Gillock

NFMC 1991-1994

According to the Merriam-Webster dictionary, *trepak* is "a fiery, Ukrainian folk dance performed by men featuring the leg-flinging prisiadka." Gillock's arrangement of Tchaikovsky's famous piece from *The Nutcracker* will require dexterity and a solid technique. Personally, I find the Primo and Secondo parts equally challenging. Marked *molto vivace*, this duet is bold, dramatic and a definite crowd pleaser.

The Chase

SECONDO

Carolyn Miller
and David Engle

Allegro moderato

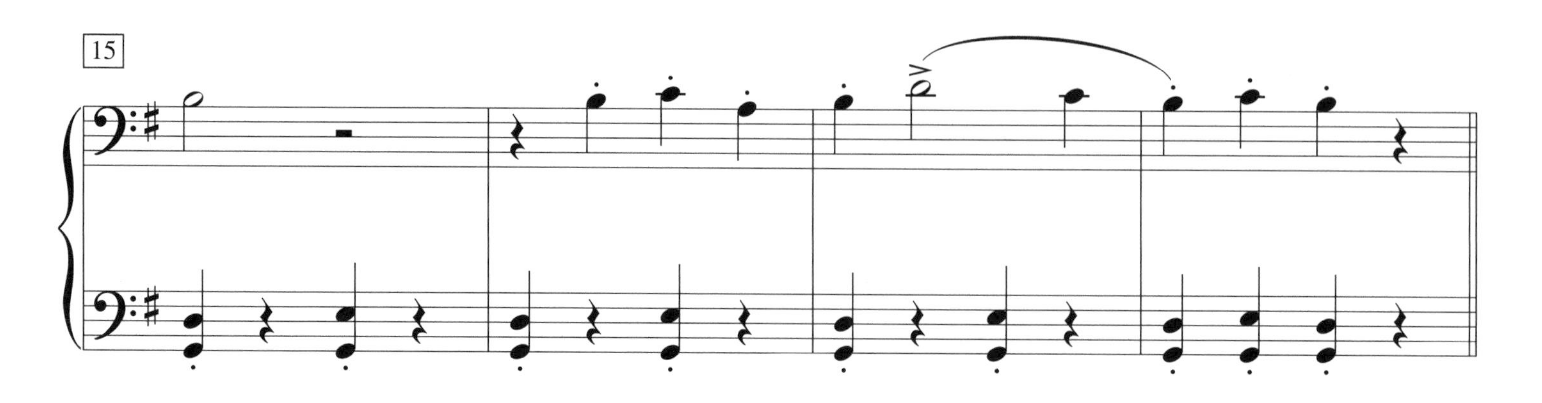

The Chase

PRIMO

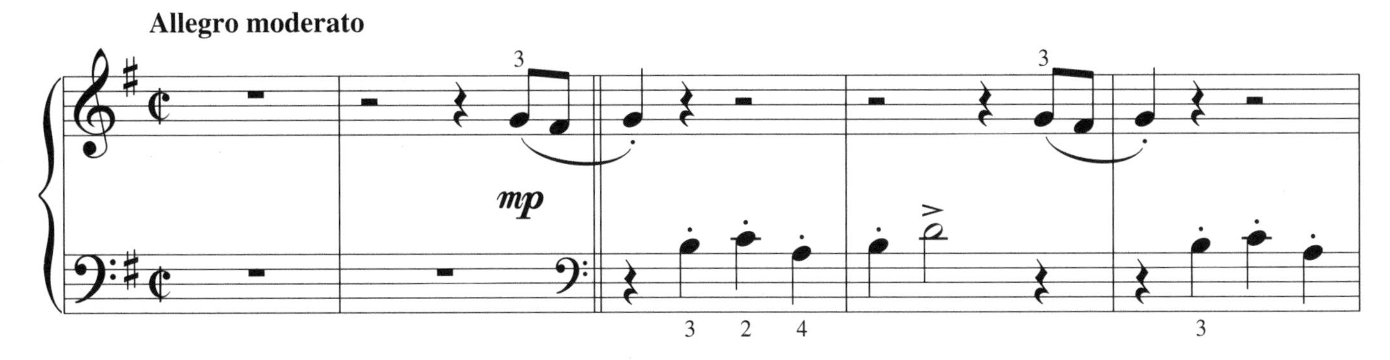

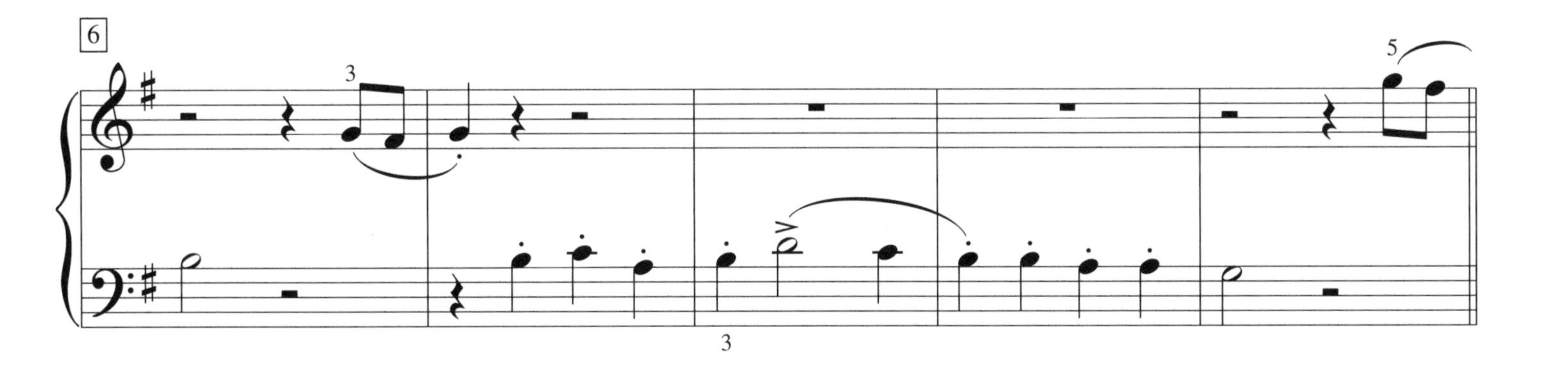

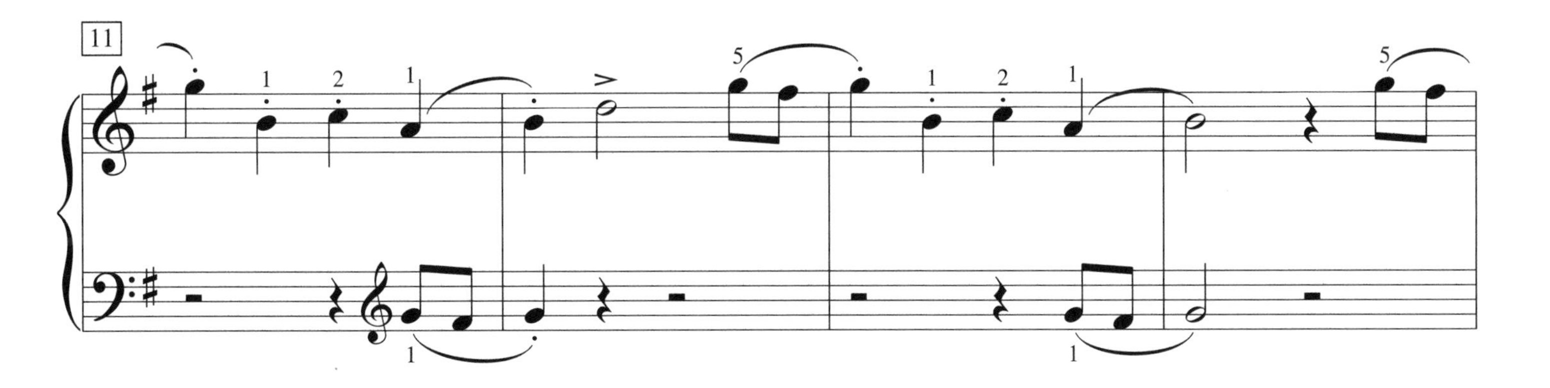

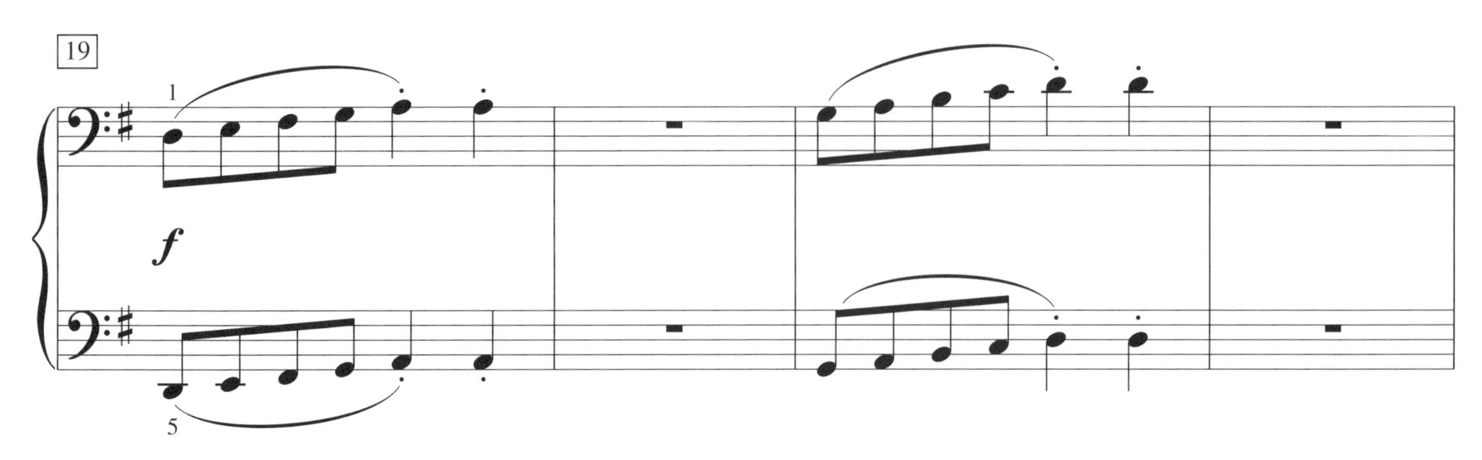
19
1
f
5

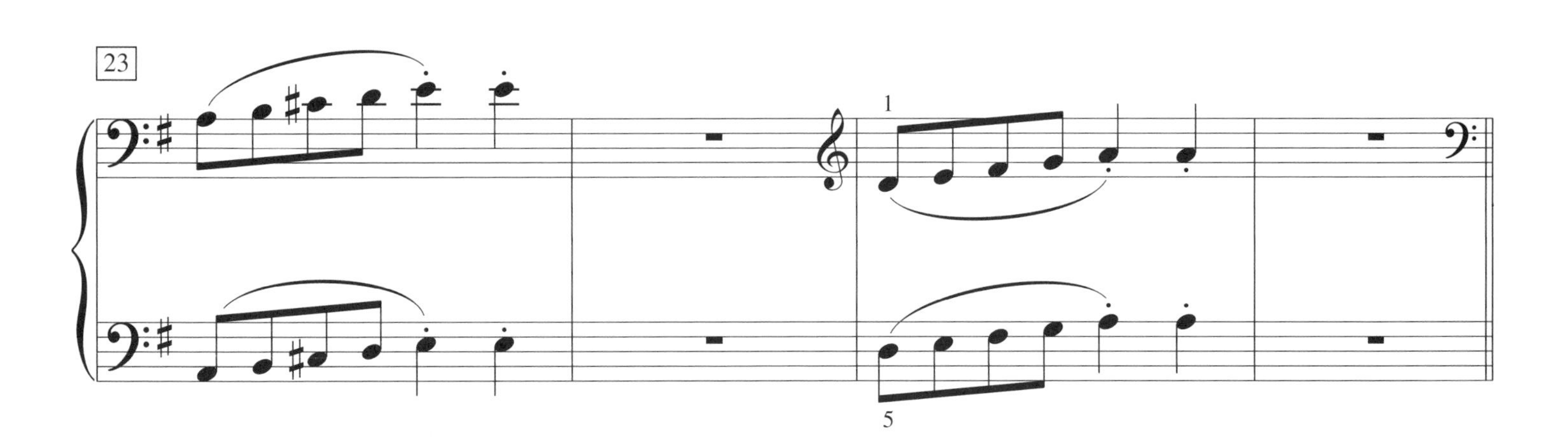
23
1
5

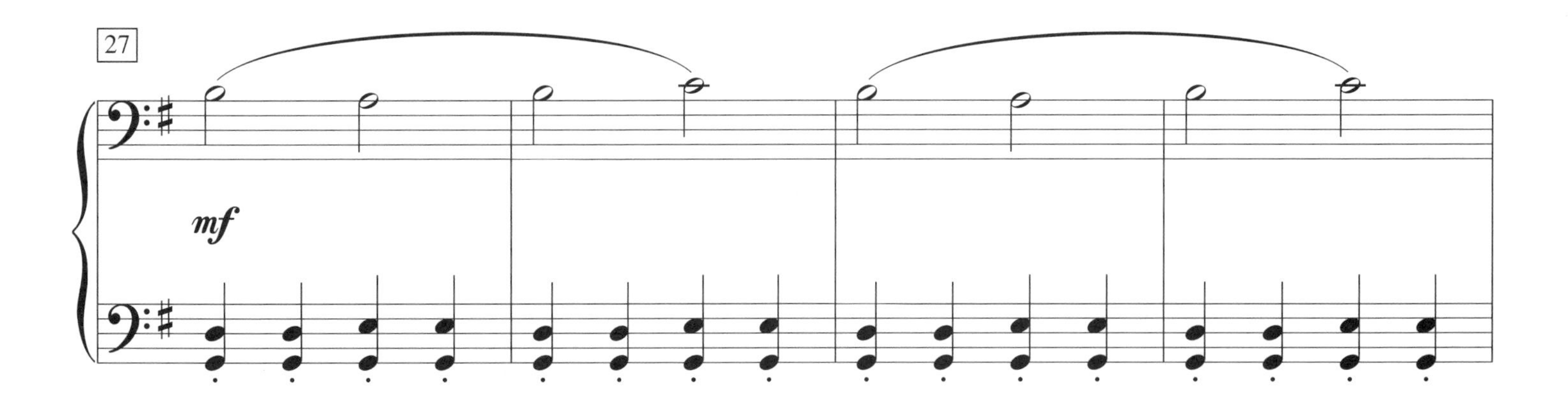
27
mf

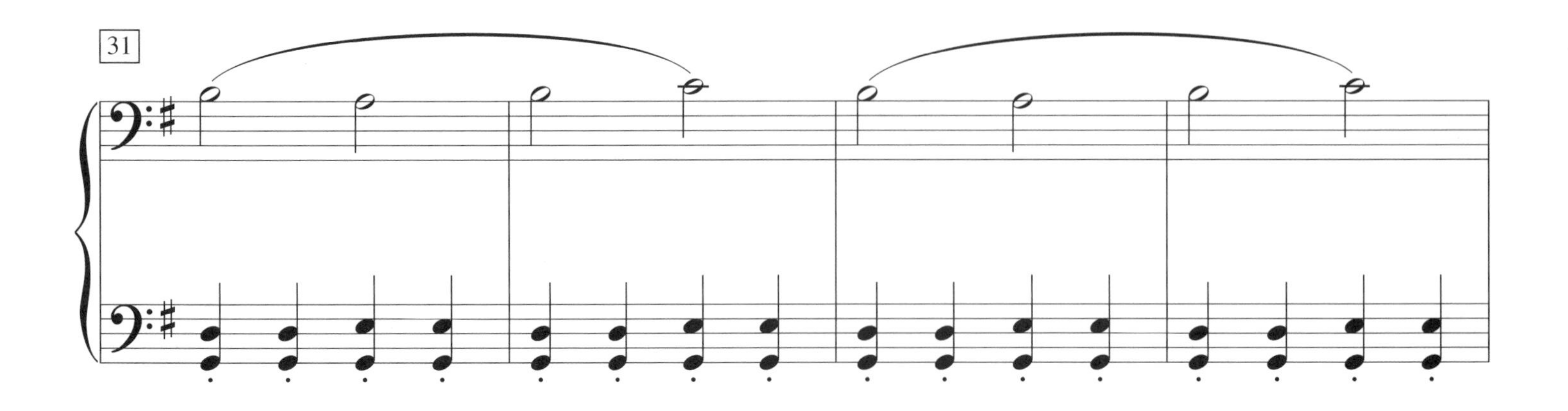
31

PRIMO

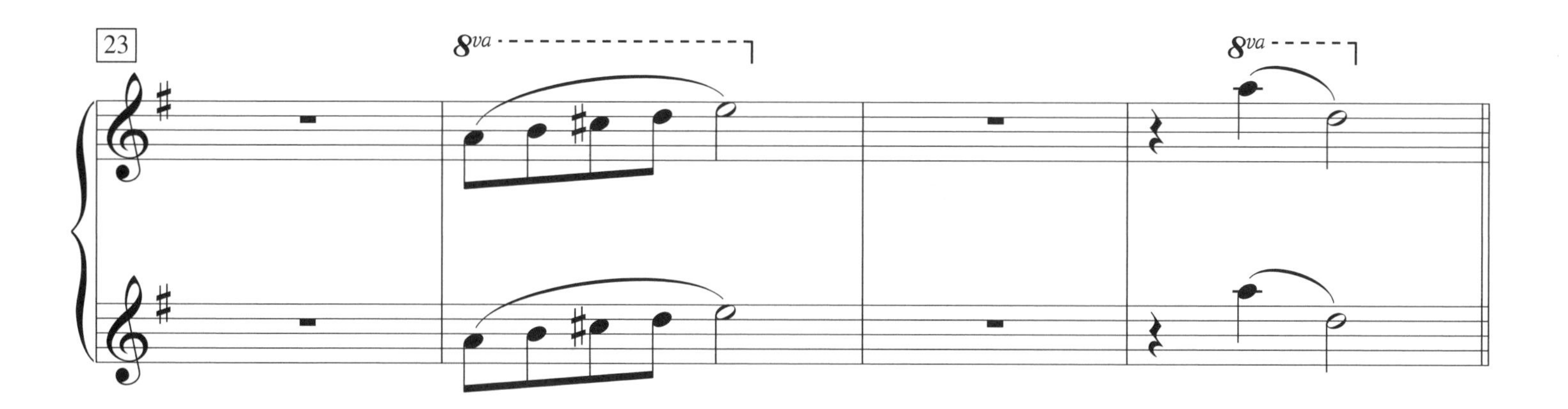

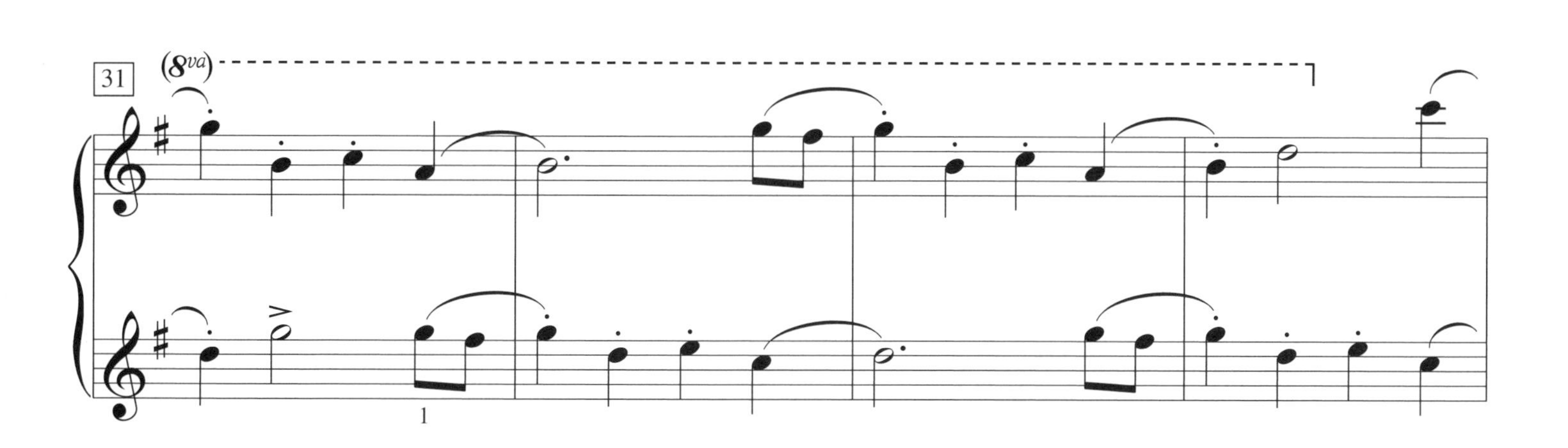

SECONDO

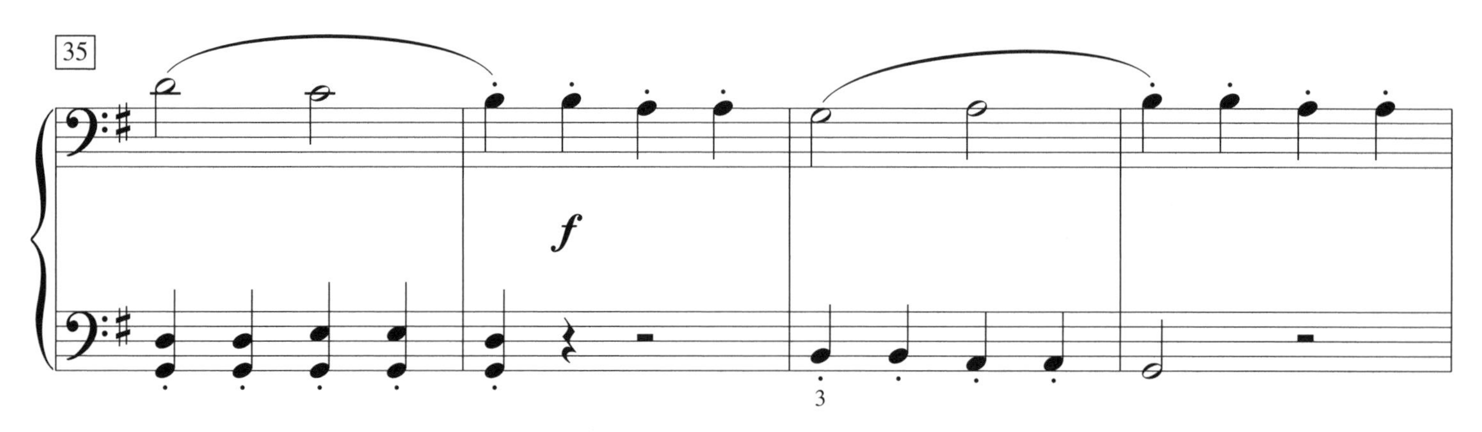

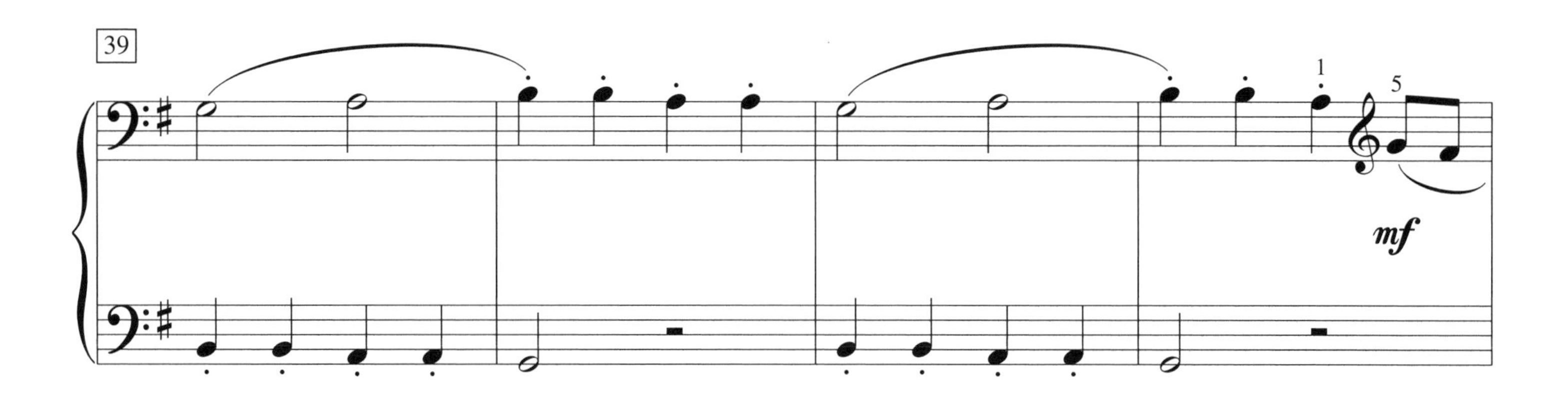

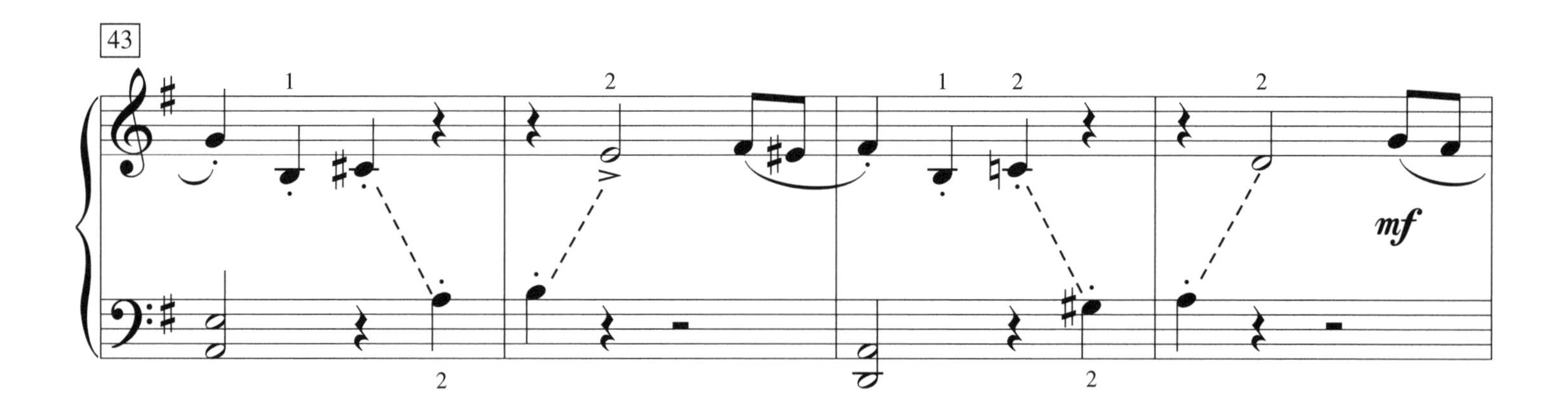

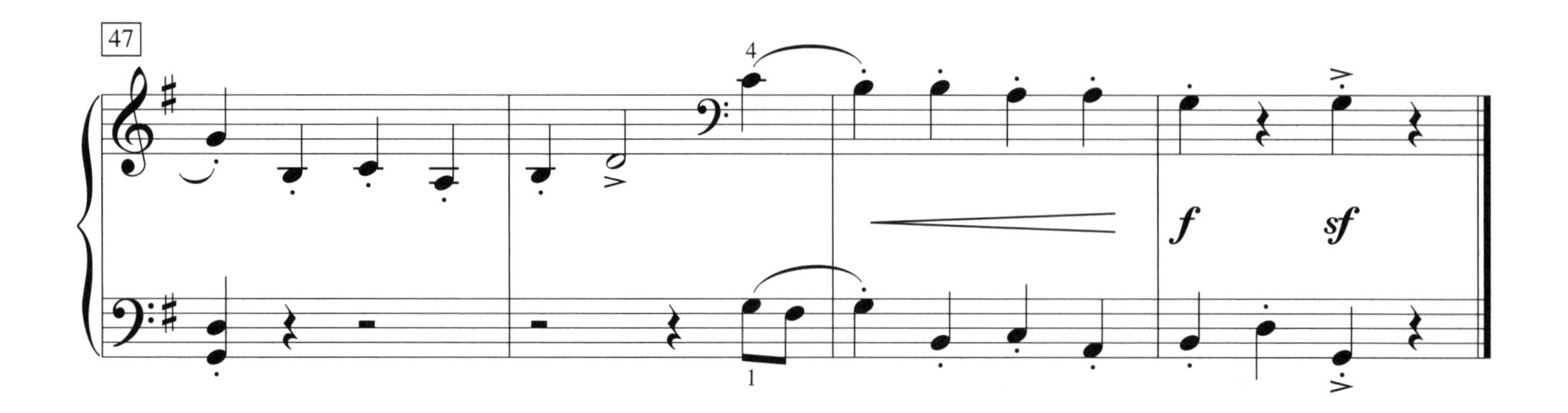

PRIMO

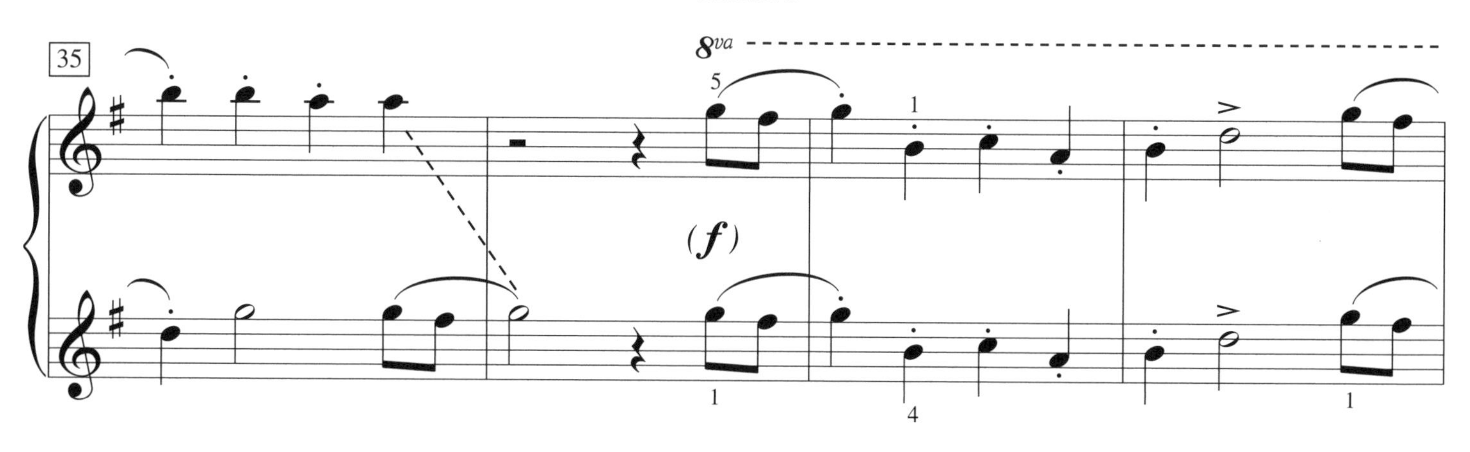

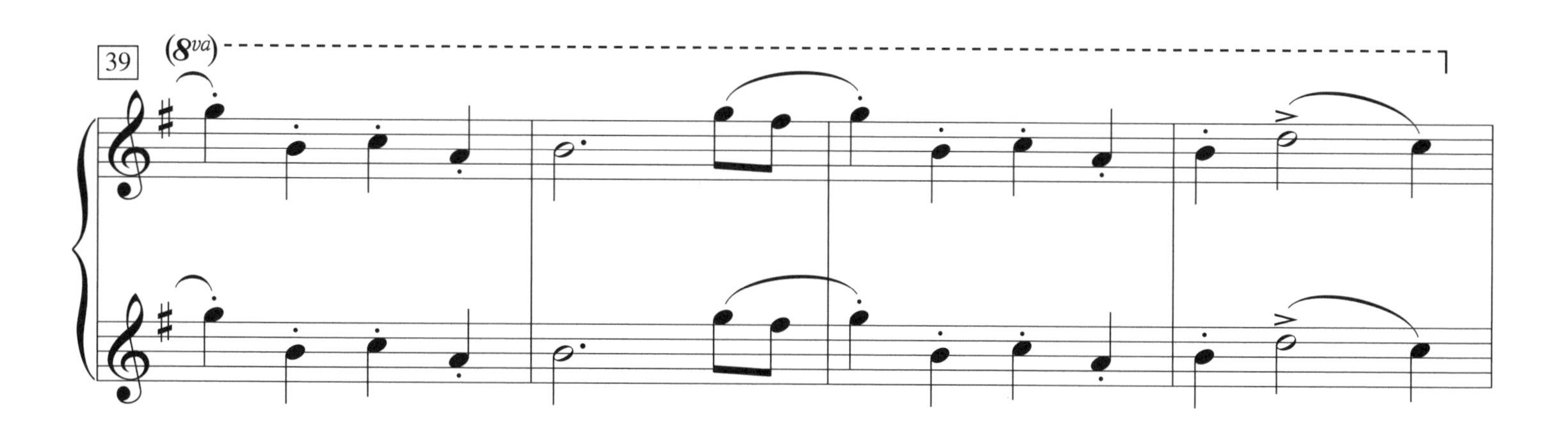

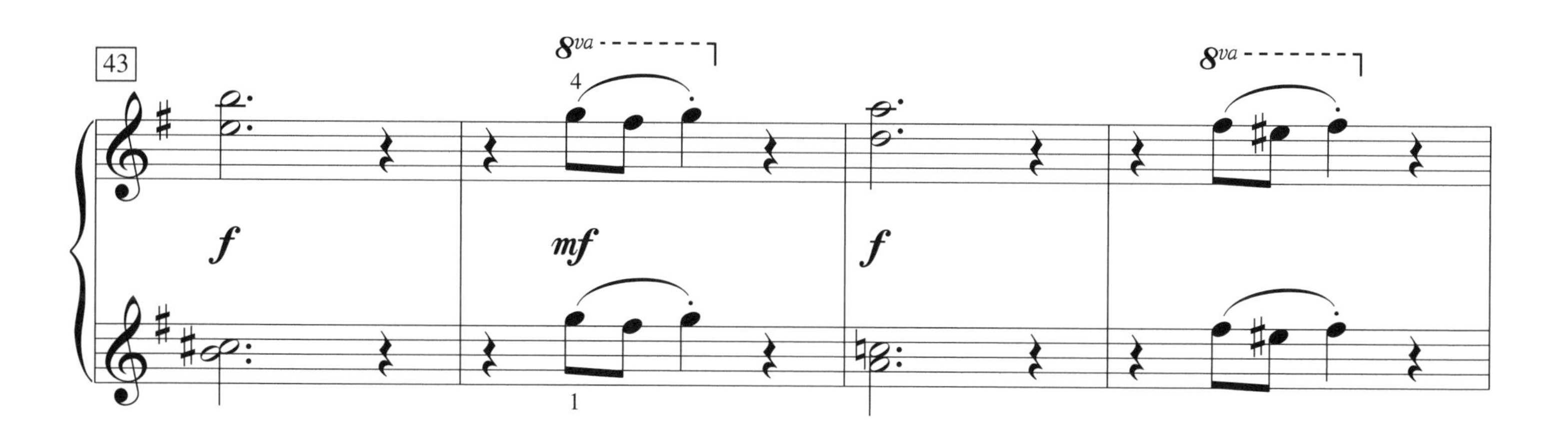

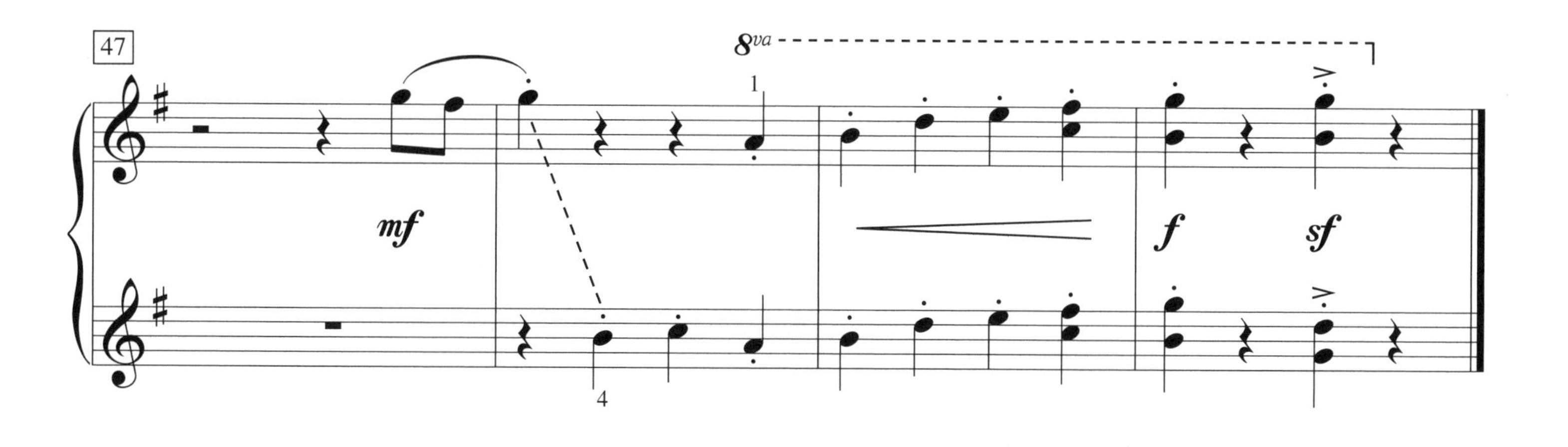

Pinwheels

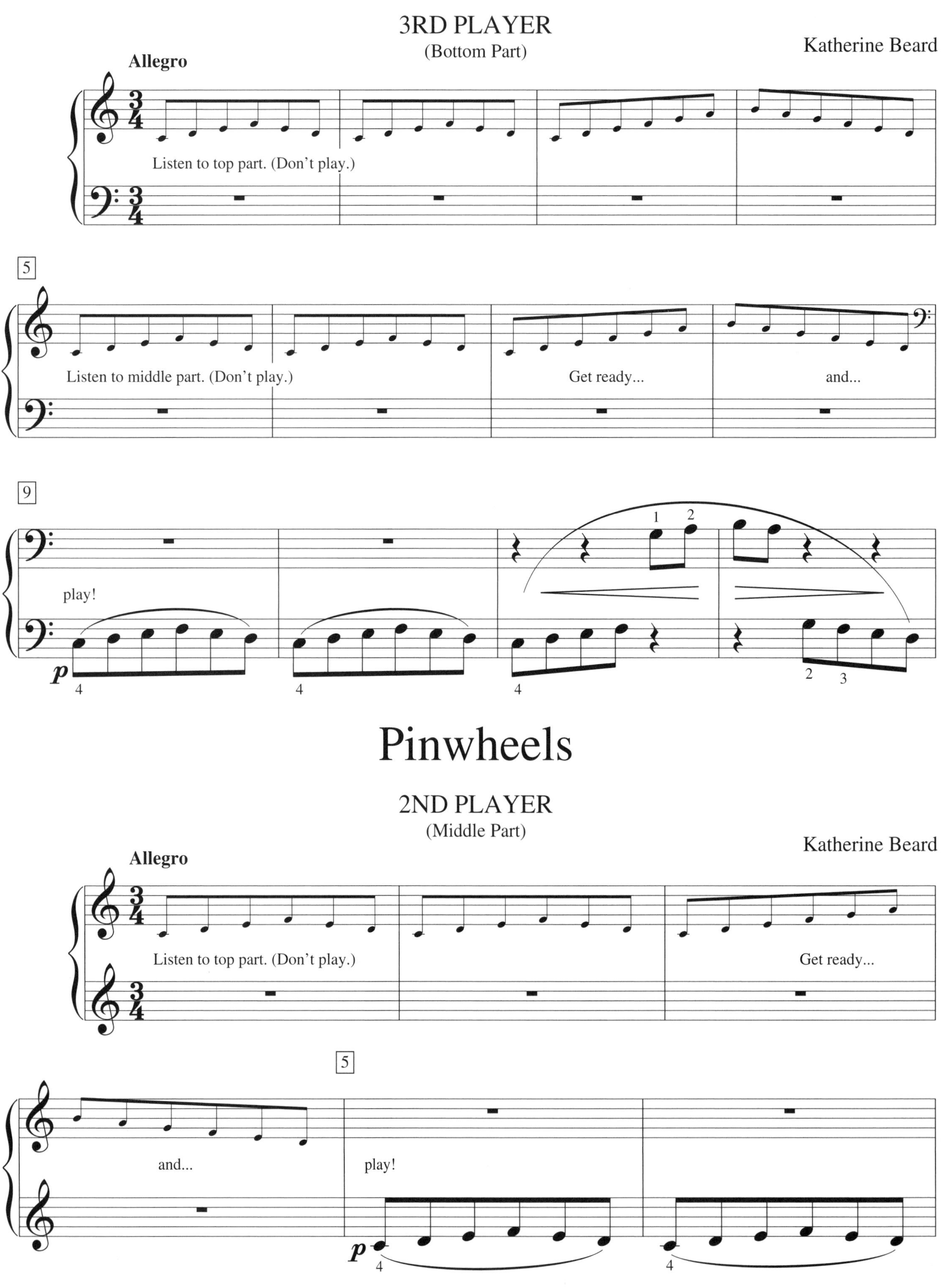
3RD PLAYER
(Bottom Part)
Katherine Beard
Allegro
Listen to top part. (Don't play.)
5
Listen to middle part. (Don't play.)
Get ready...
and...
9
play!
p
Pinwheels
2ND PLAYER
(Middle Part)
Katherine Beard
Allegro
Listen to top part. (Don't play.)
Get ready...
5
and...
play!
p

Pinwheels

1ST PLAYER
(Top Part)

Katherine Beard

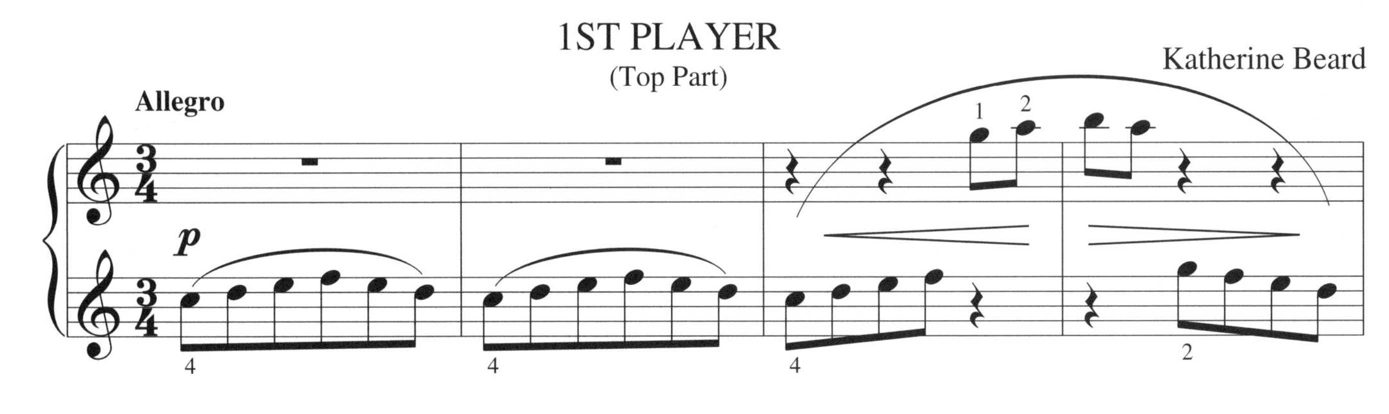

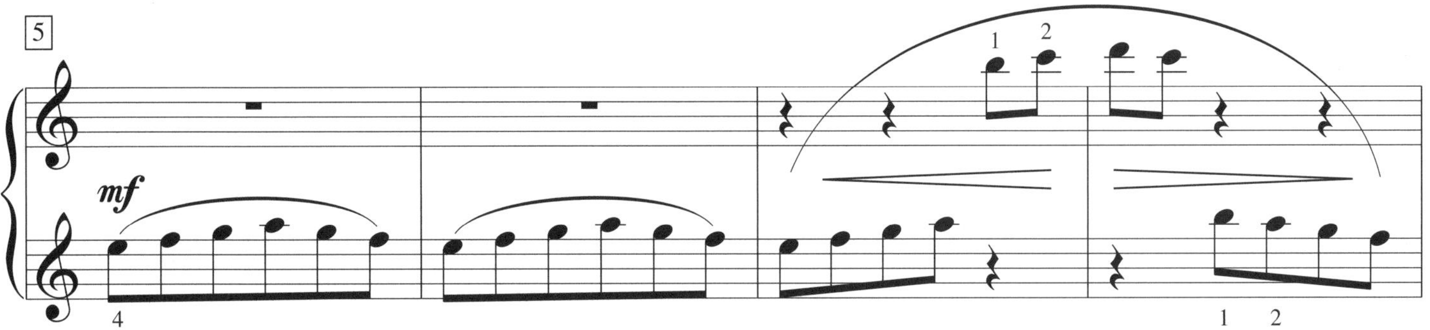

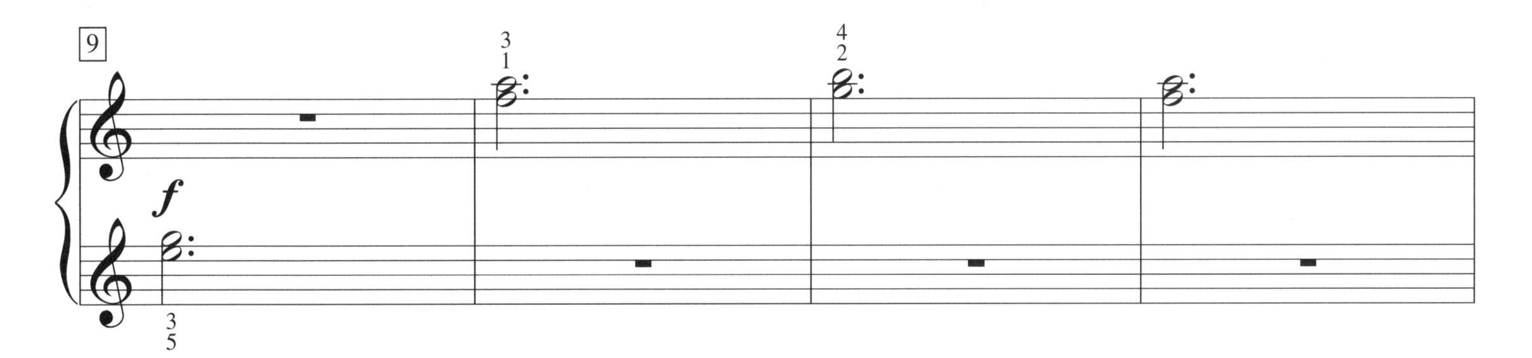

2ND PLAYER

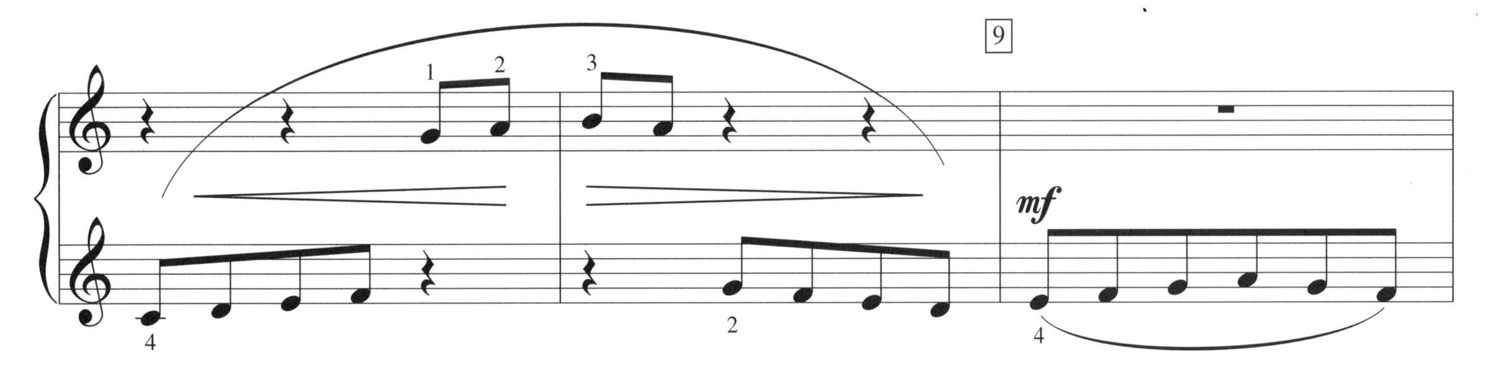

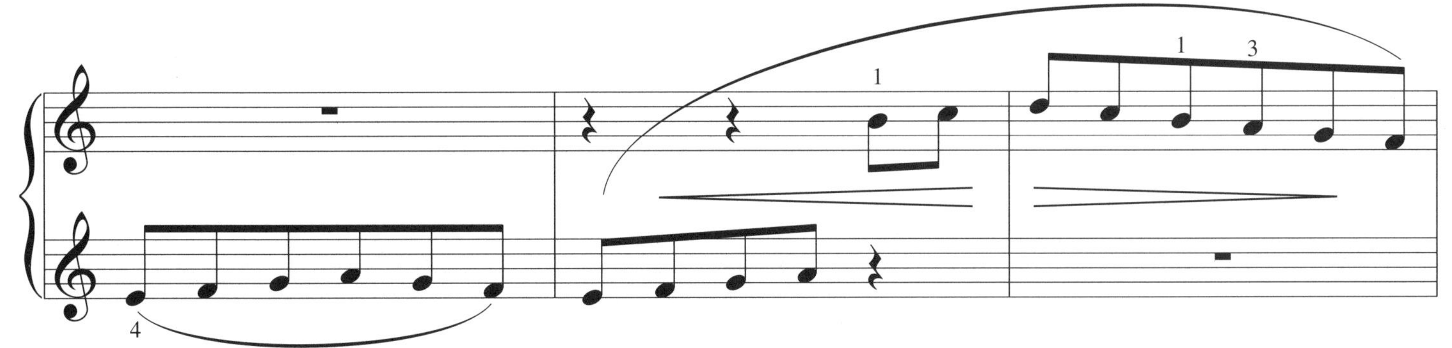

3RD PLAYER

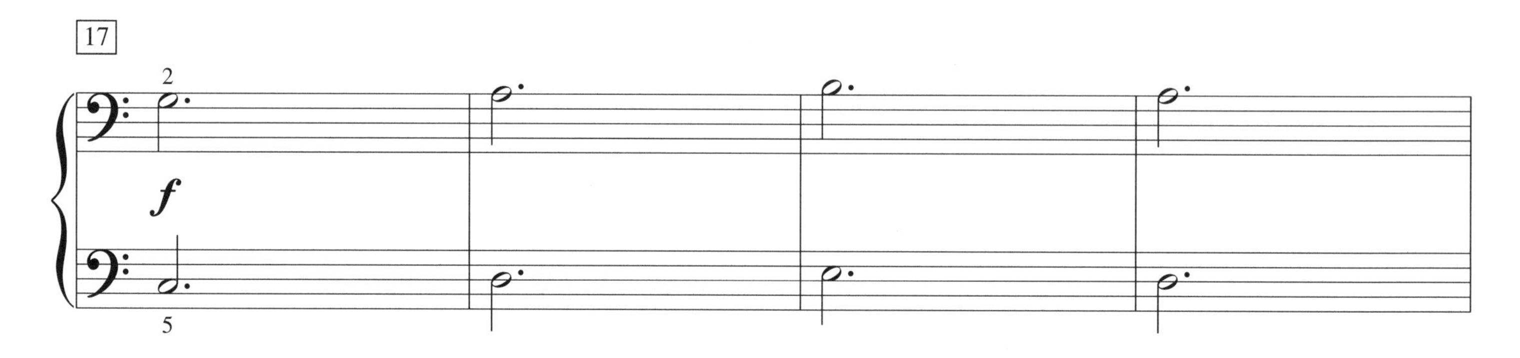

2ND PLAYER

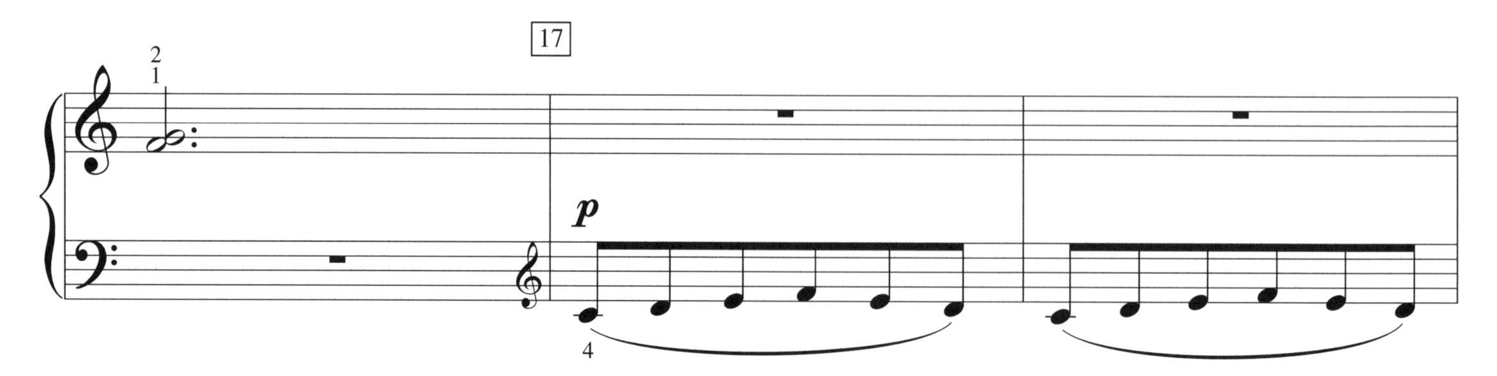

1ST PLAYER

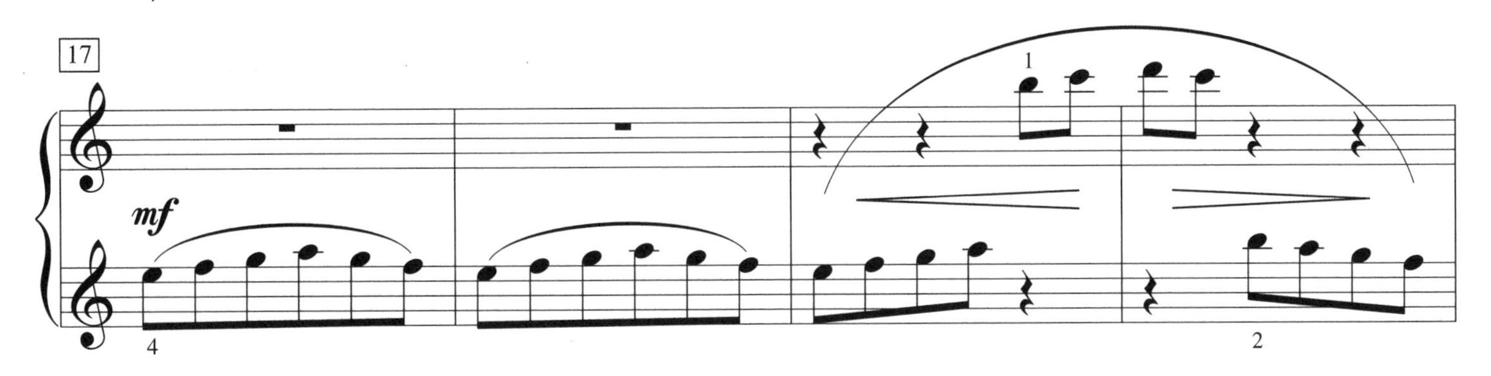

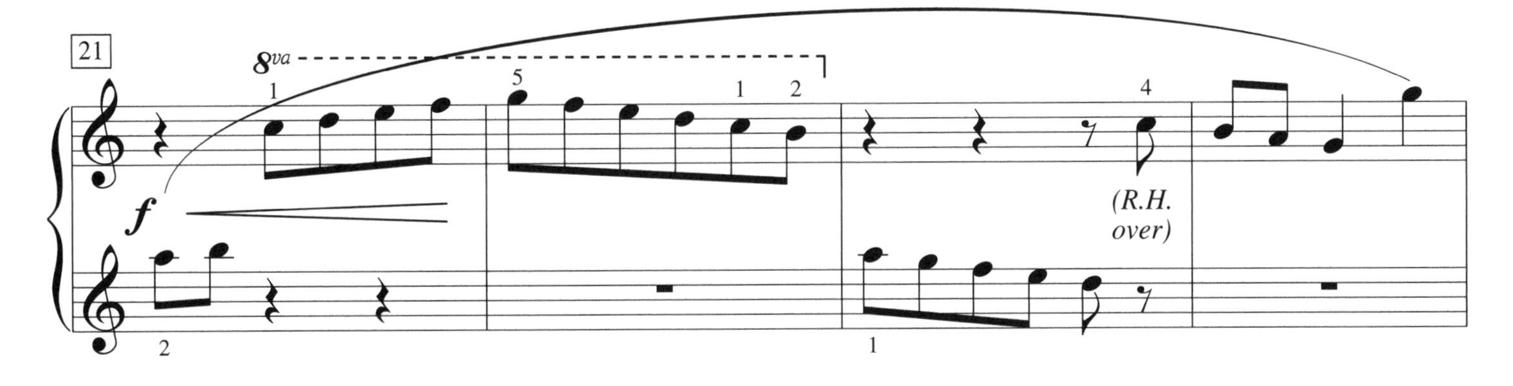

2ND PLAYER

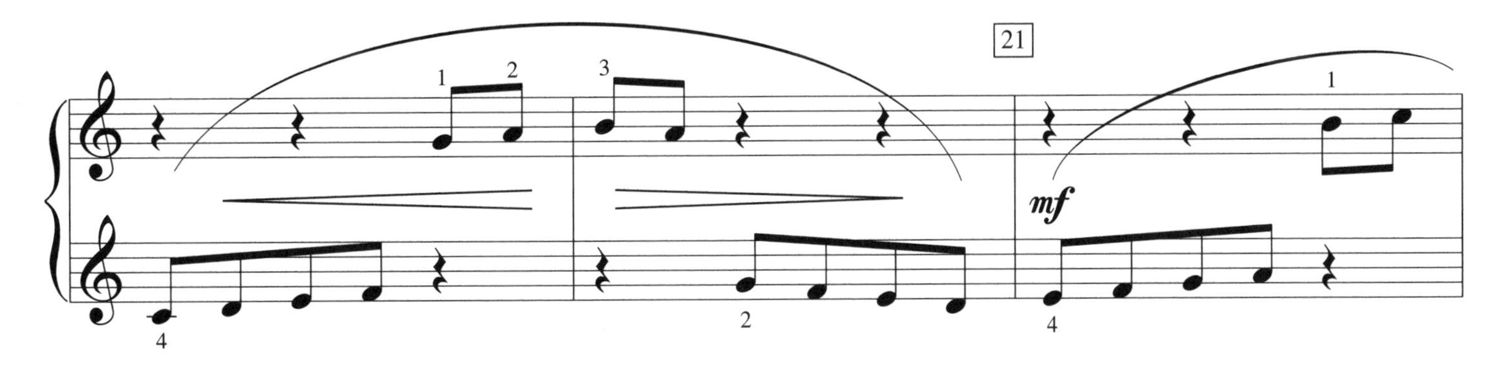

3RD PLAYER

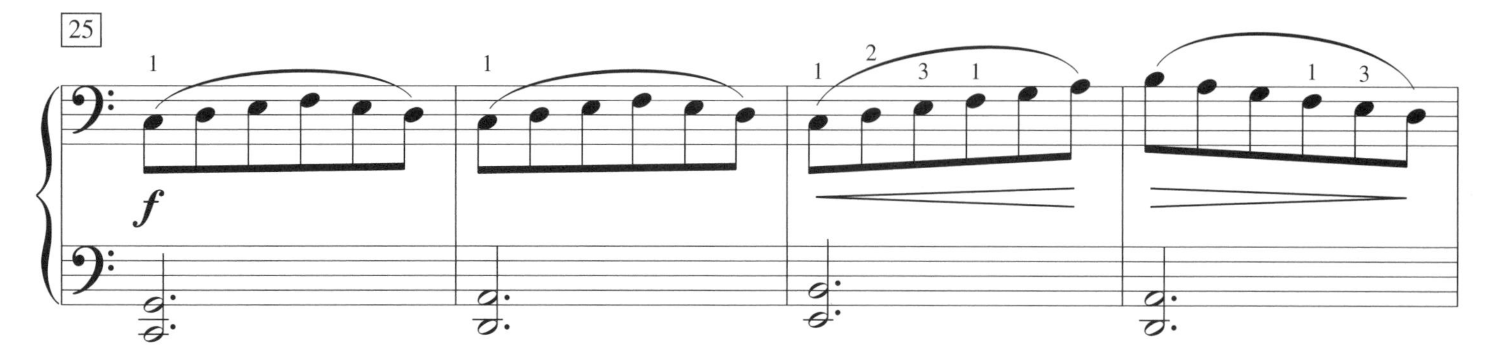

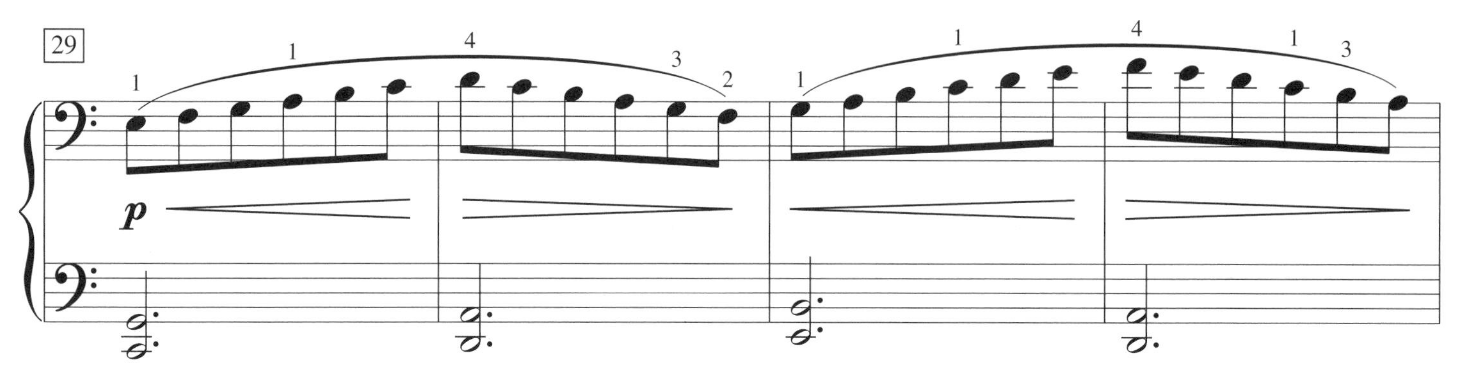

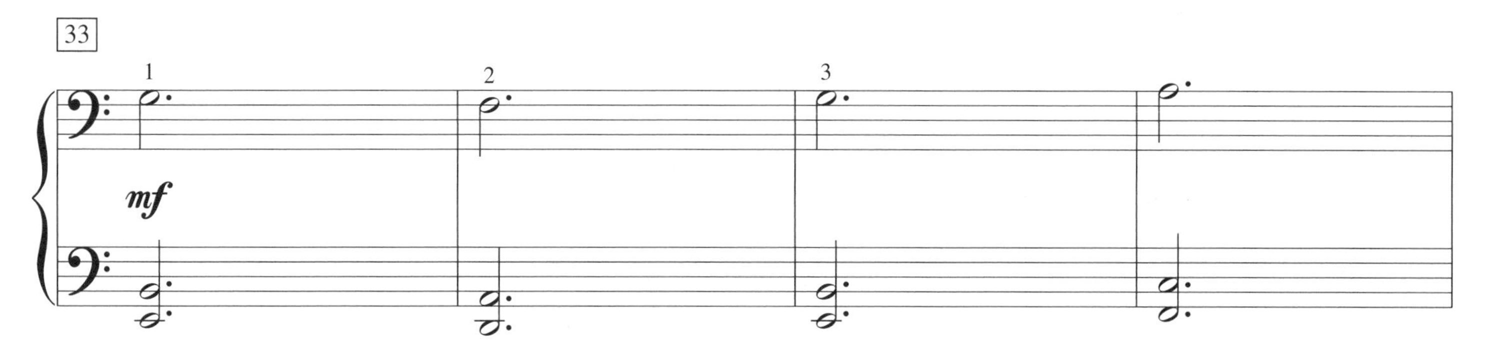

2ND PLAYER

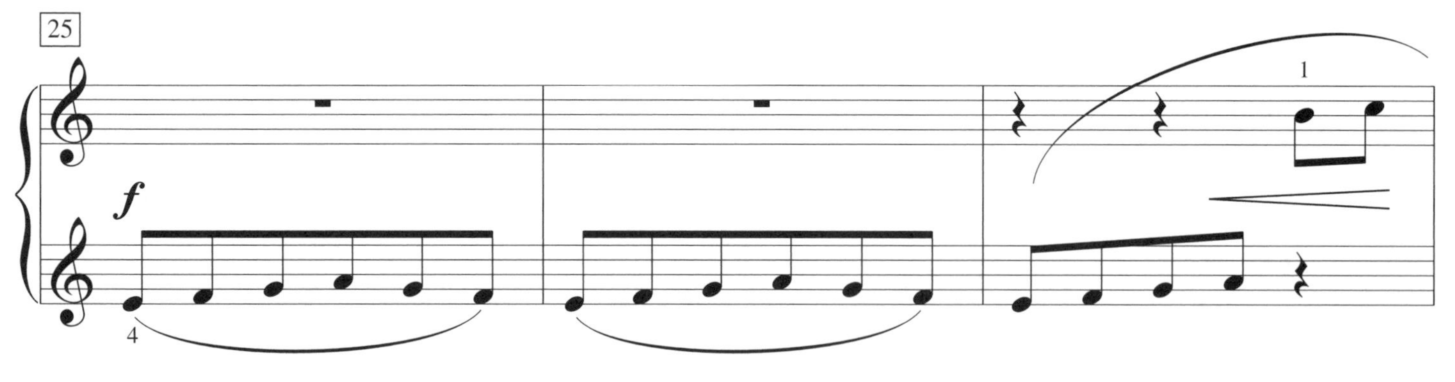

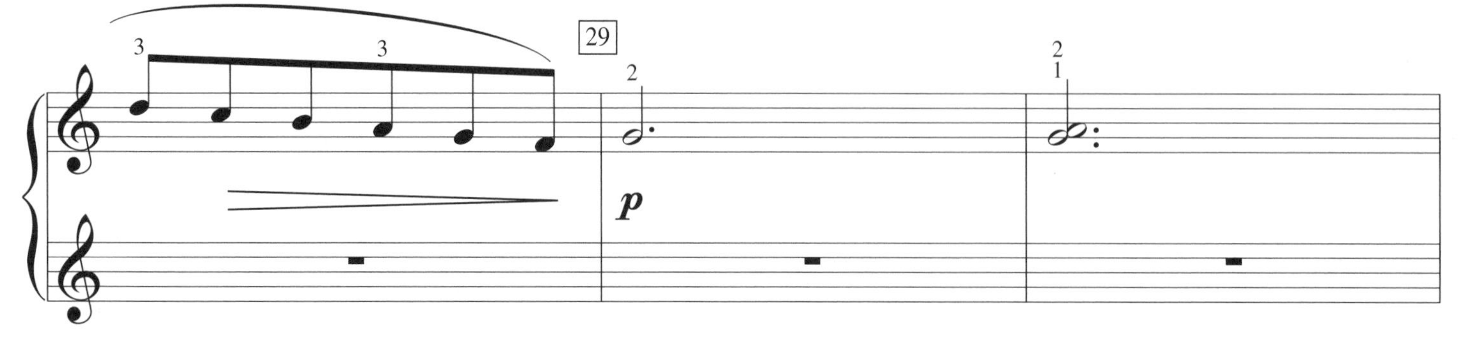

1ST PLAYER

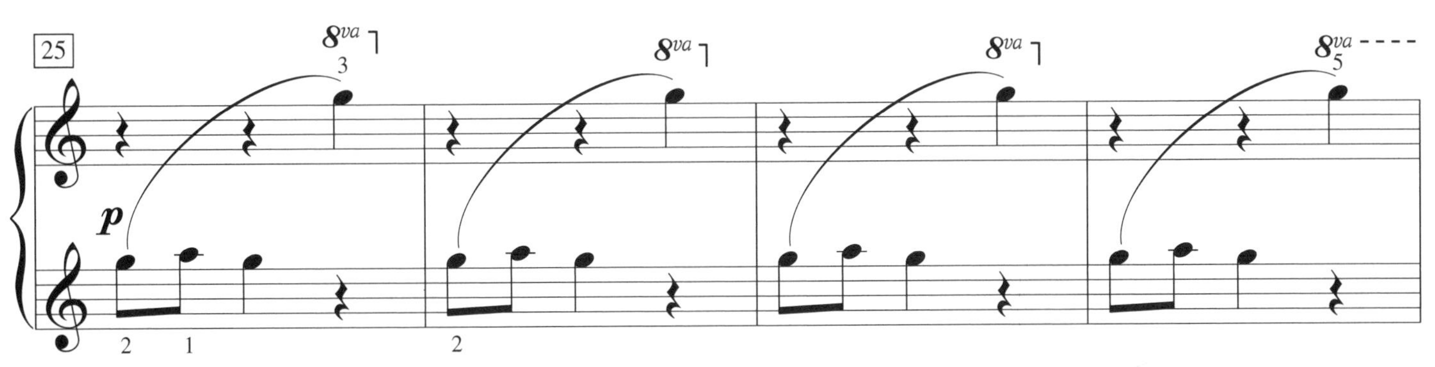

2ND PLAYER

3RD PLAYER

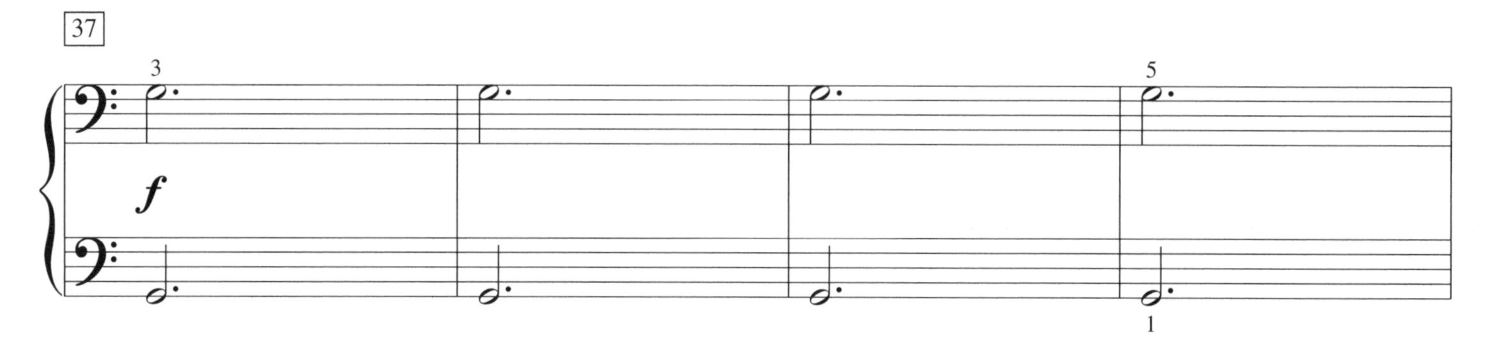

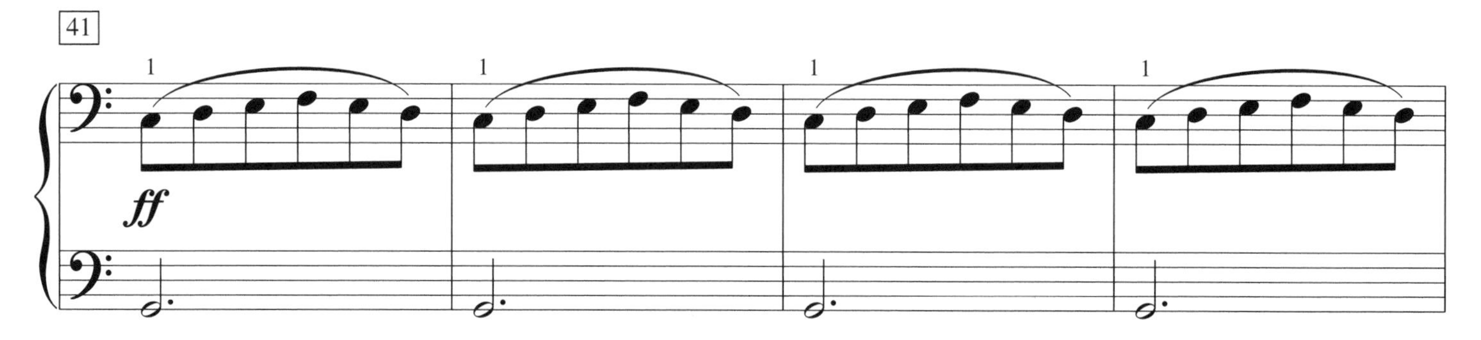

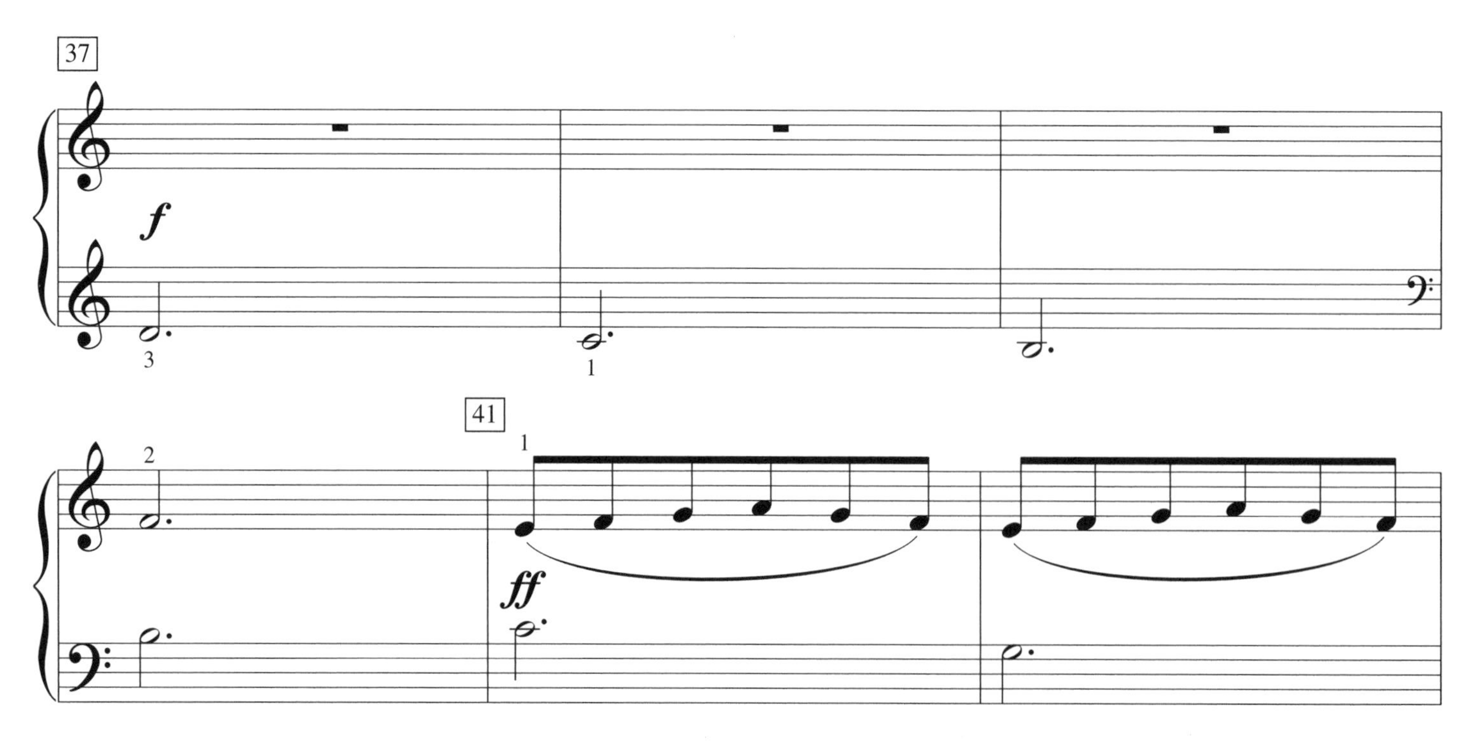

1ST PLAYER

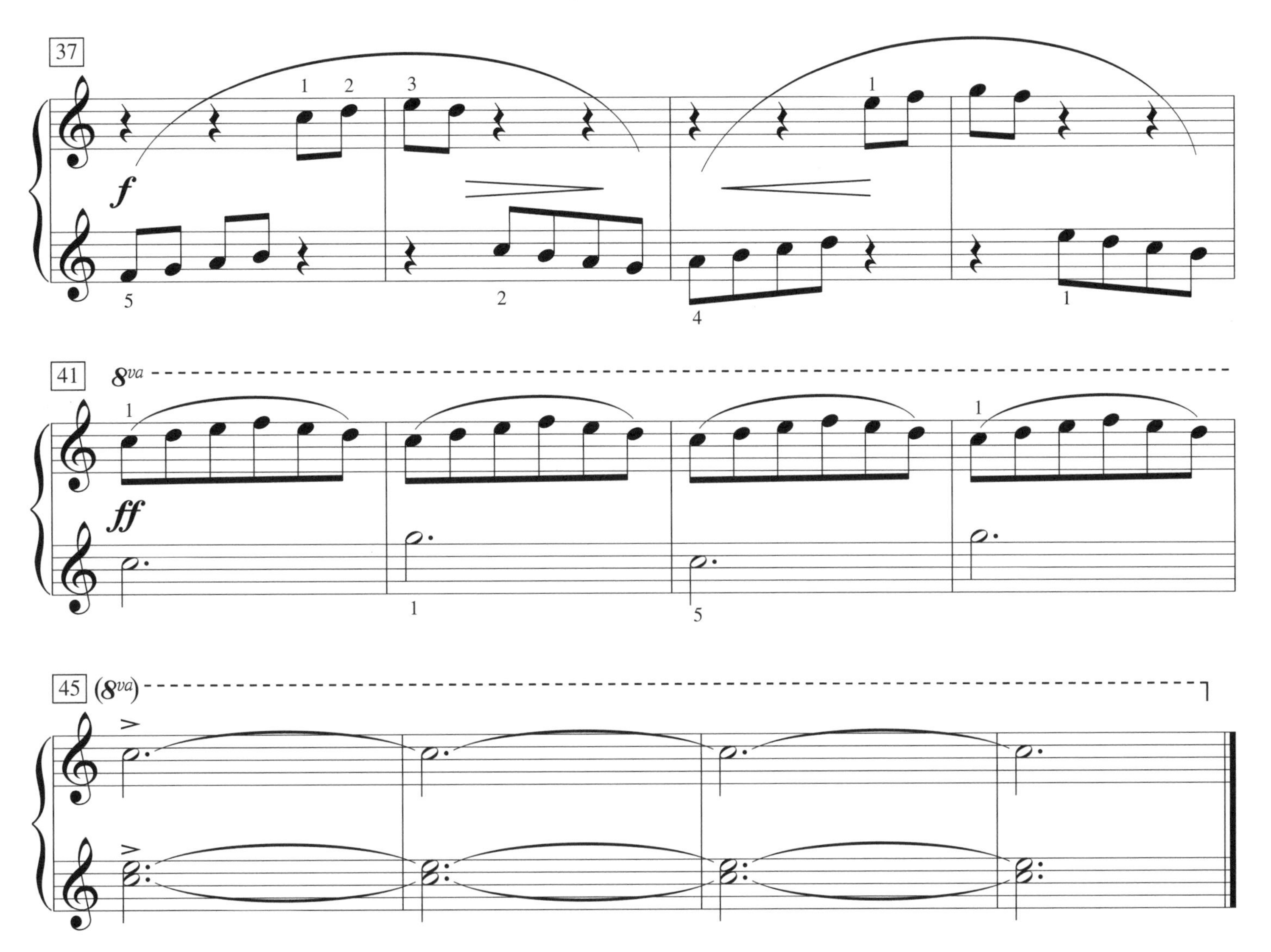

2ND PLAYER

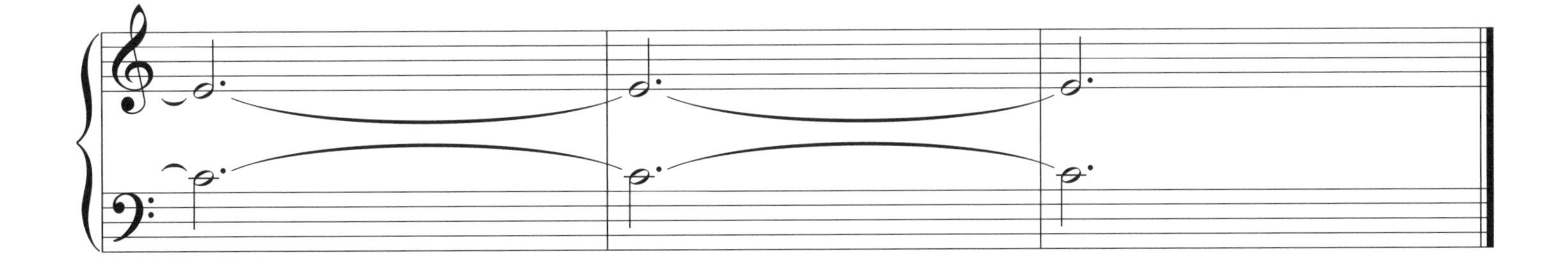

Kibbutz Capers

SECONDO

David Karp

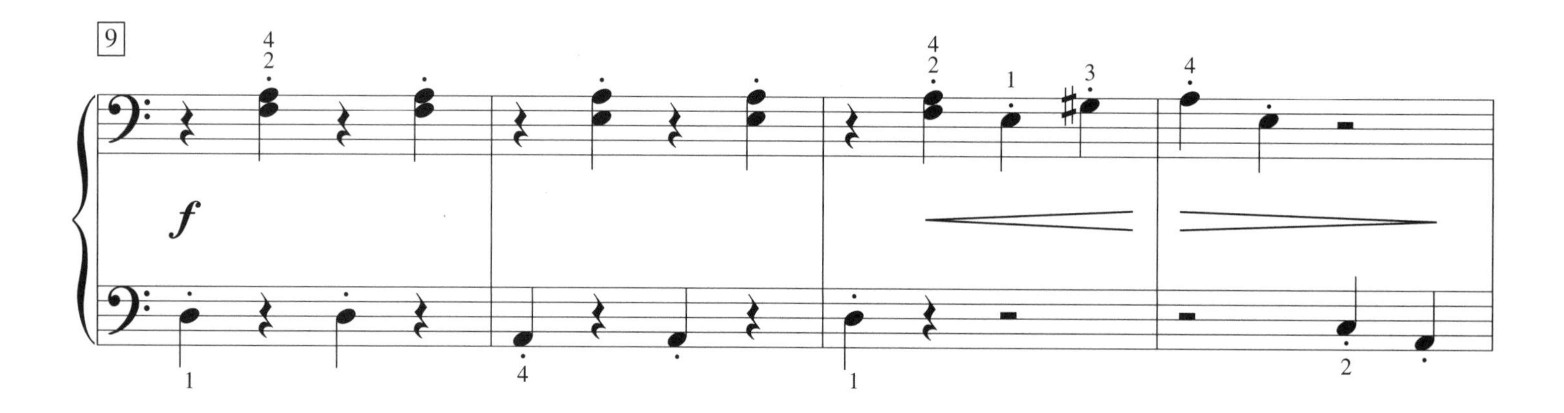

Kibbutz Capers

PRIMO

David Karp

Vivace

mf

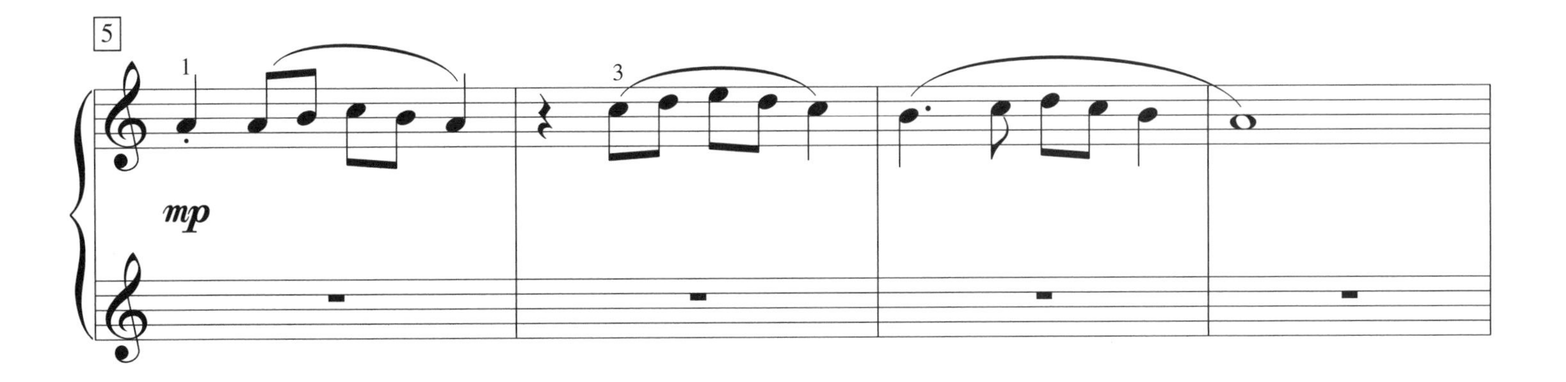

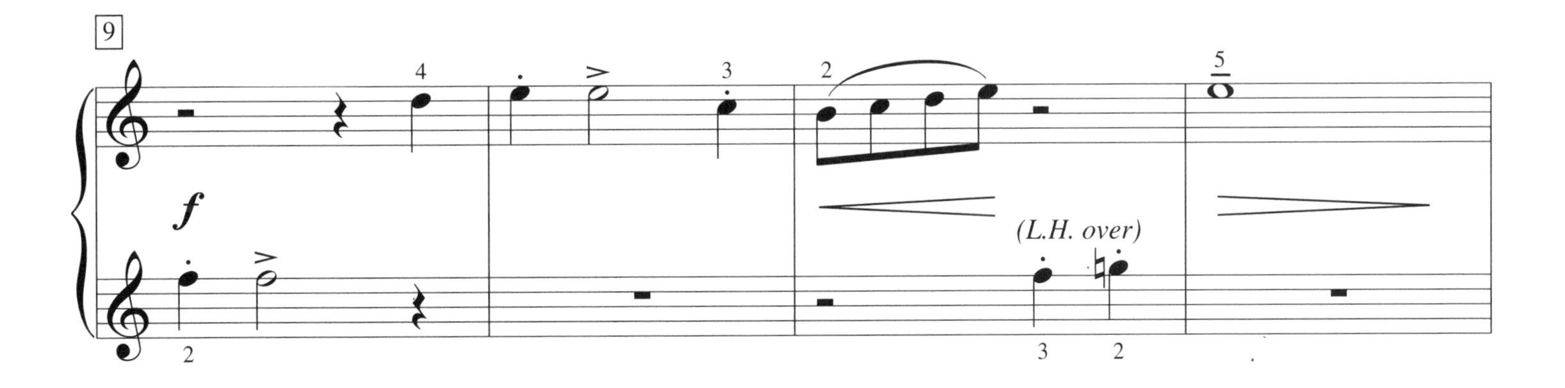

SECONDO

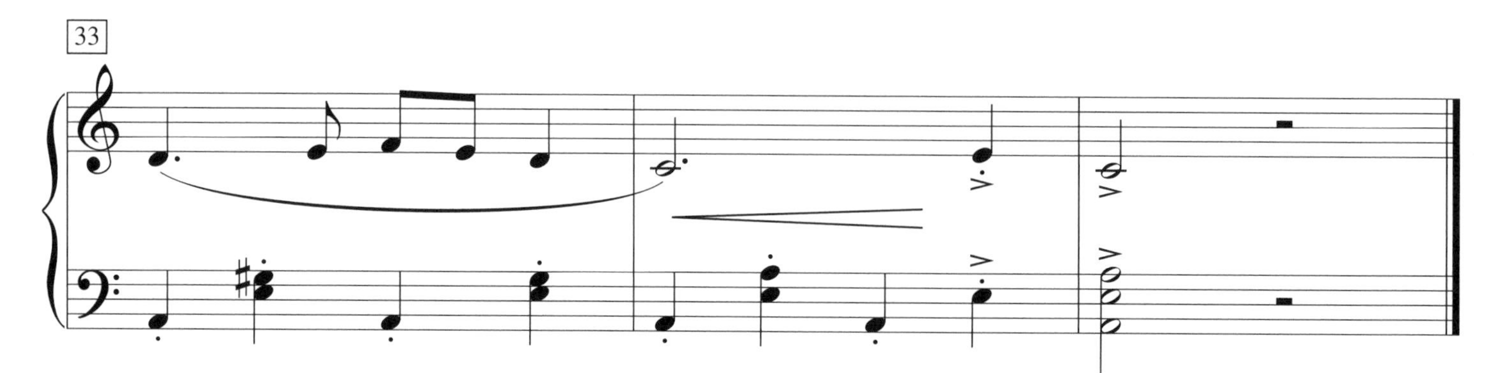

PRIMO

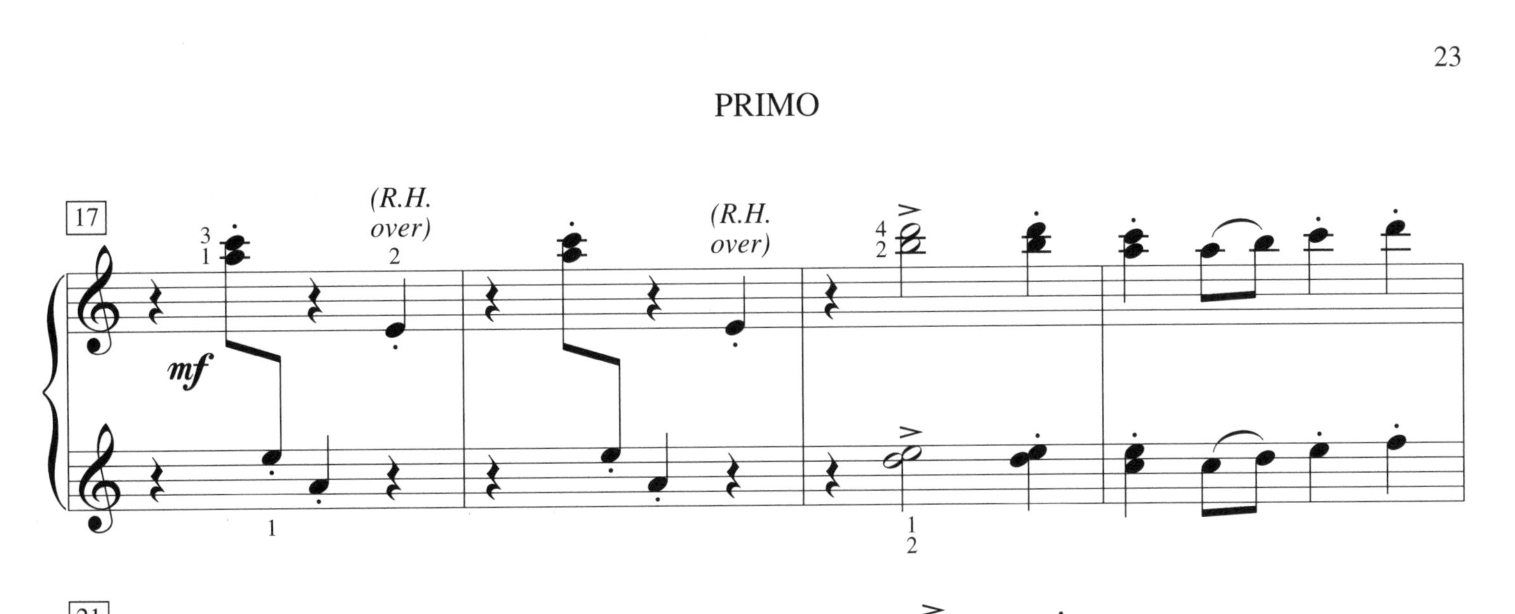

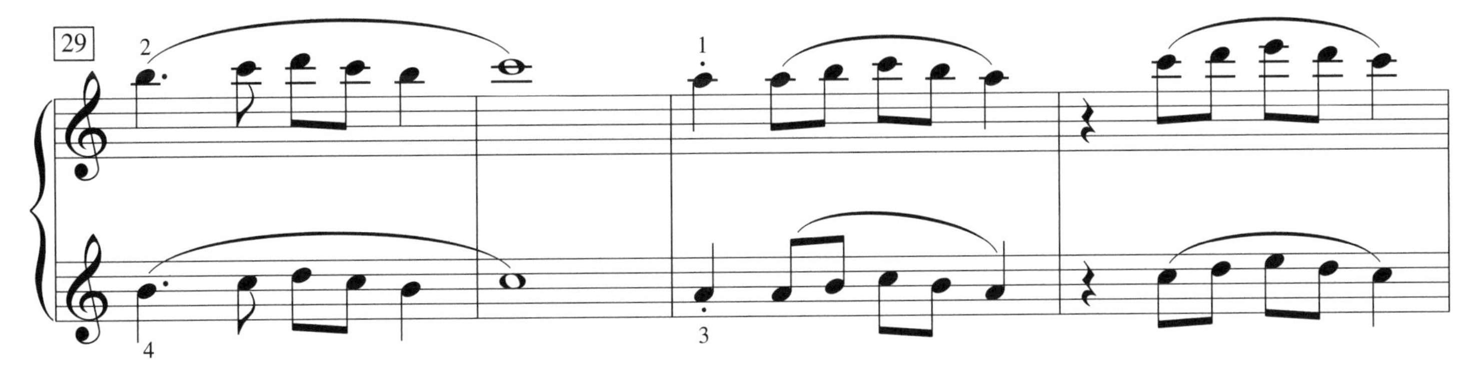

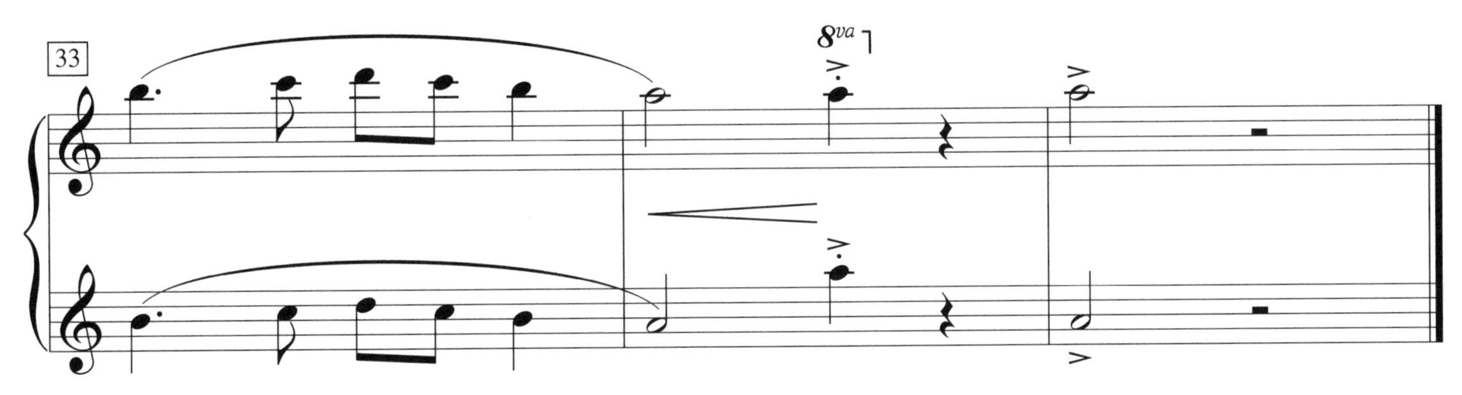

Petite Spanish Dance

SECONDO

Carolyn Miller

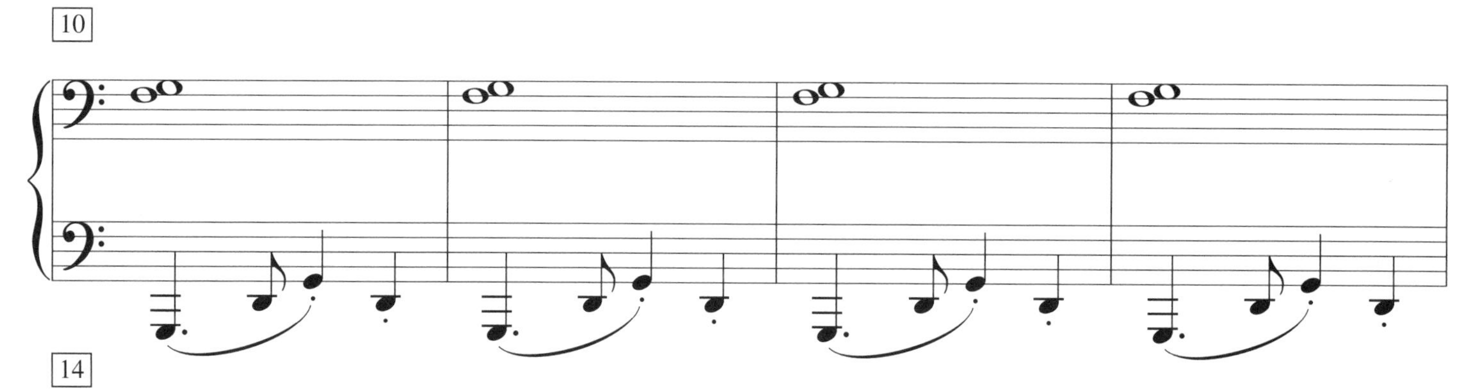

Petite Spanish Dance

PRIMO

Carolyn Miller

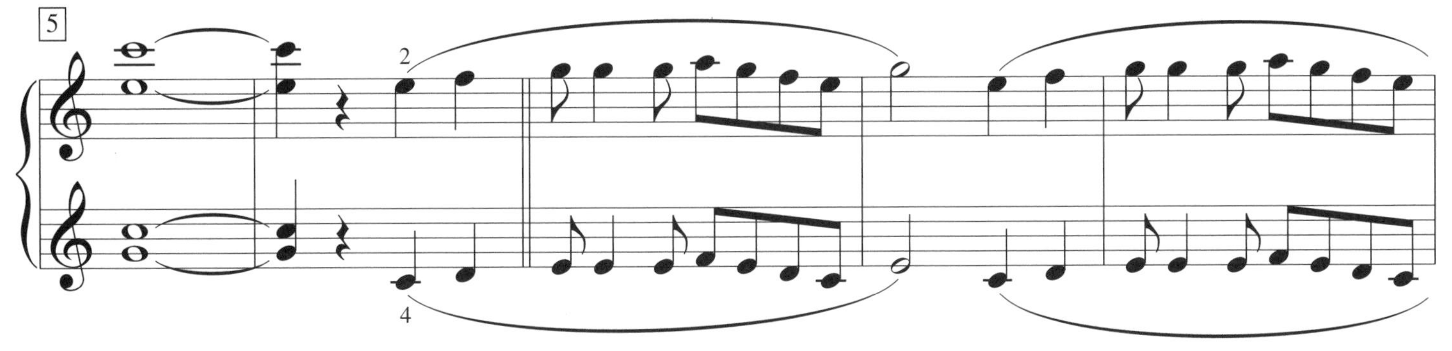

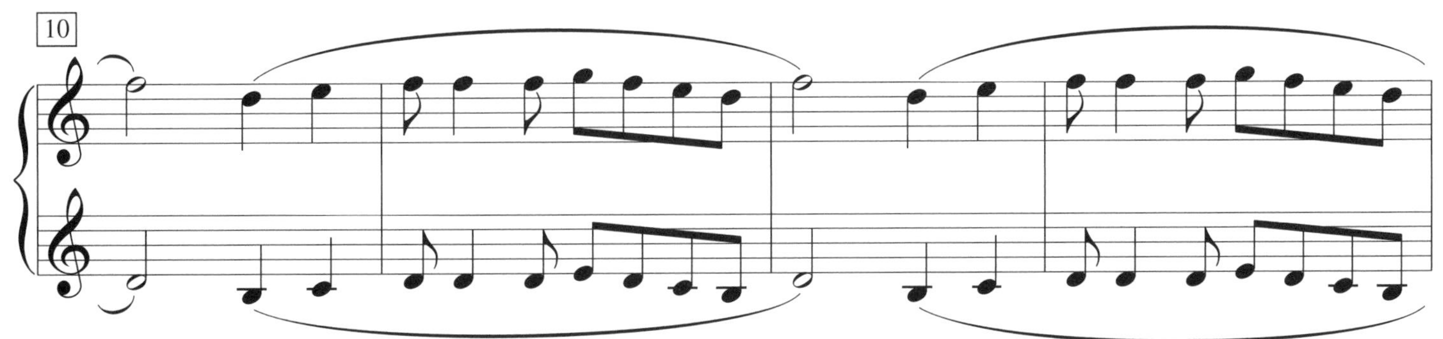

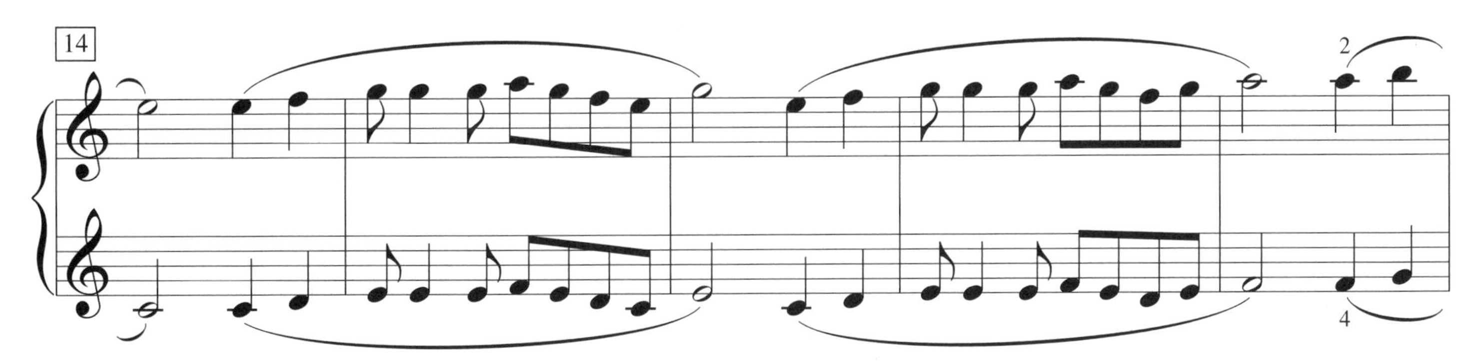

SECONDO

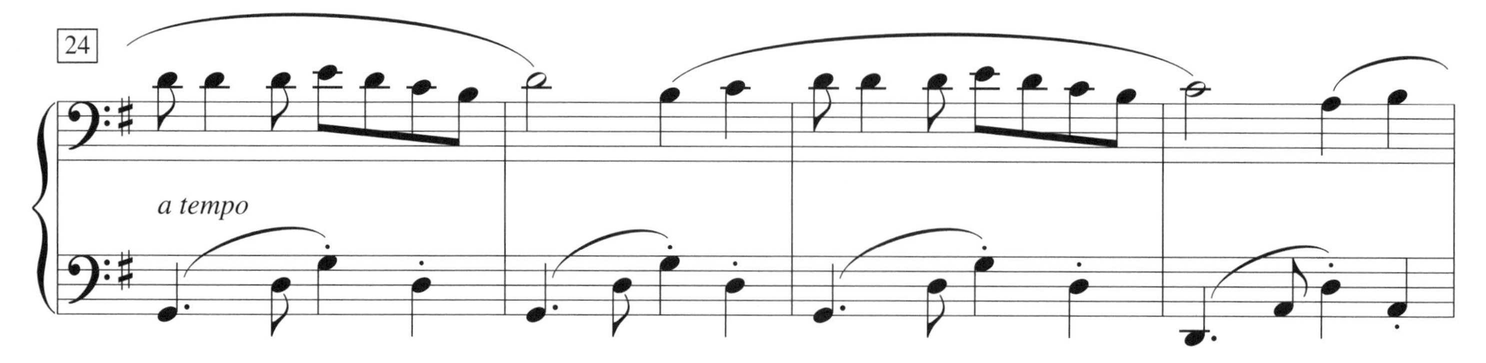

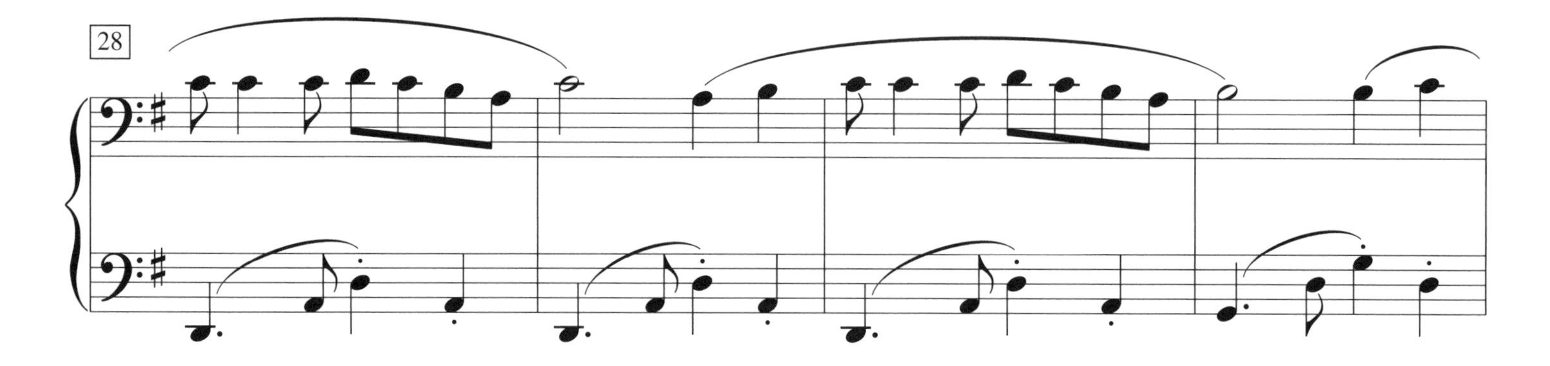

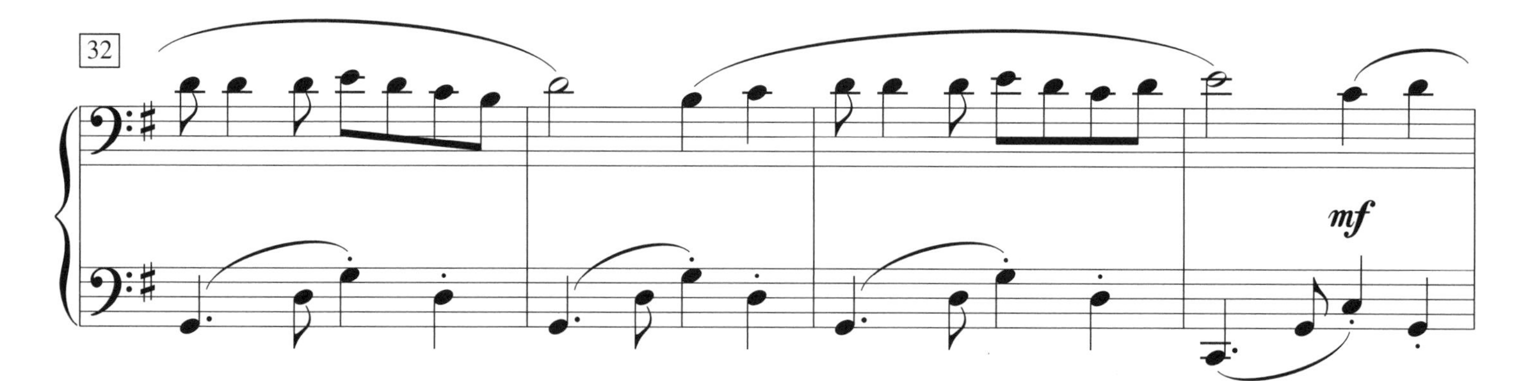

PRIMO

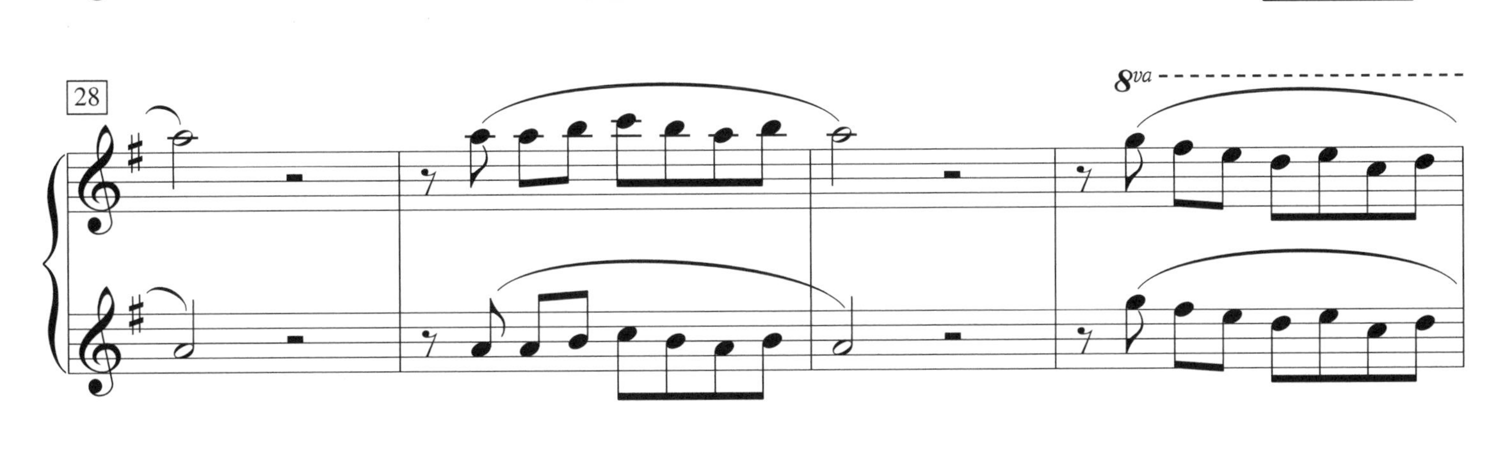

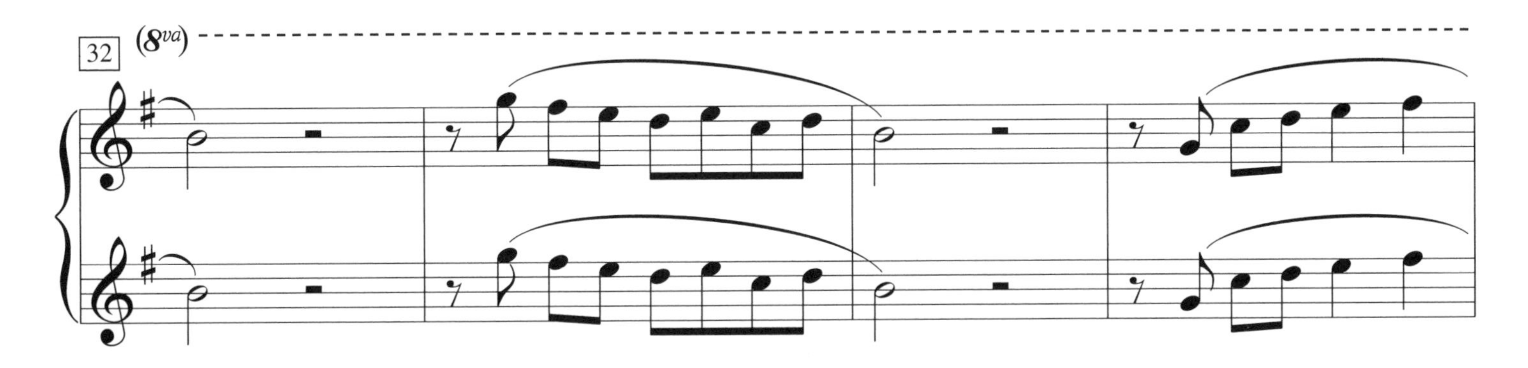

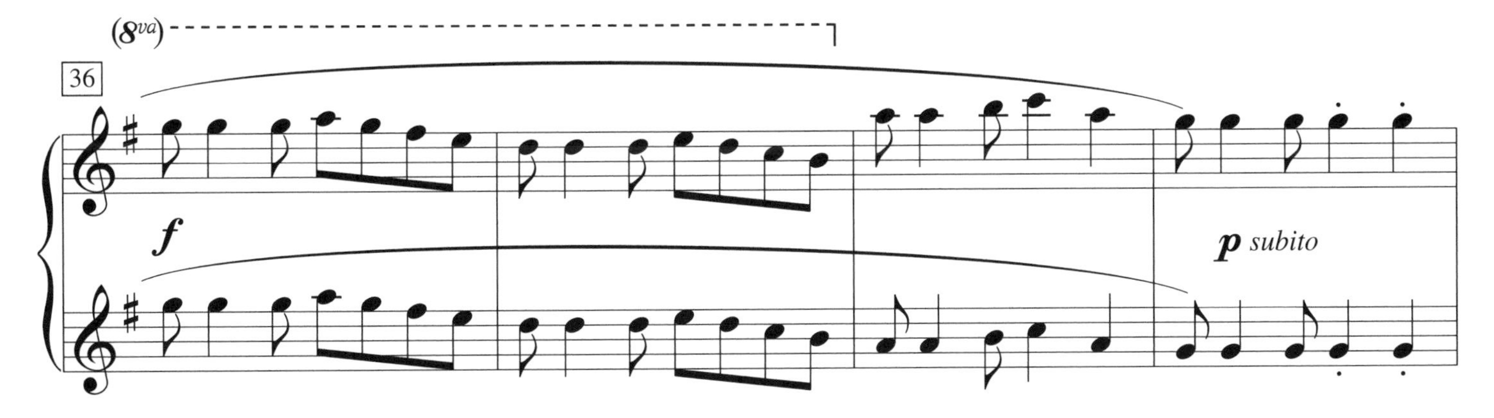

To Glenda and Gloria

Oriental Bazaar

3RD PLAYER

(Bottom Part)

William Gillock

Oriental Bazaar

2ND PLAYER

(Middle Part)

William Gillock

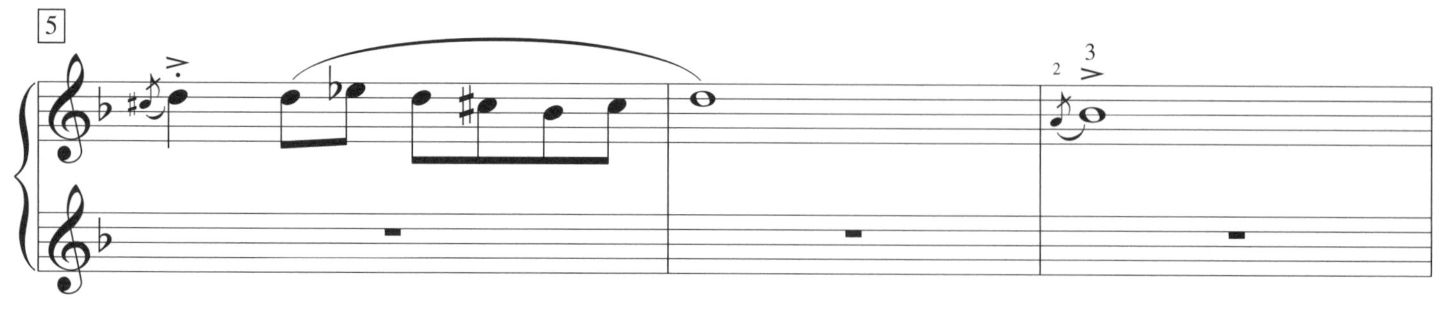

To Glenda and Gloria

Oriental Bazaar

1ST PLAYER

(Top Part)

William Gillock

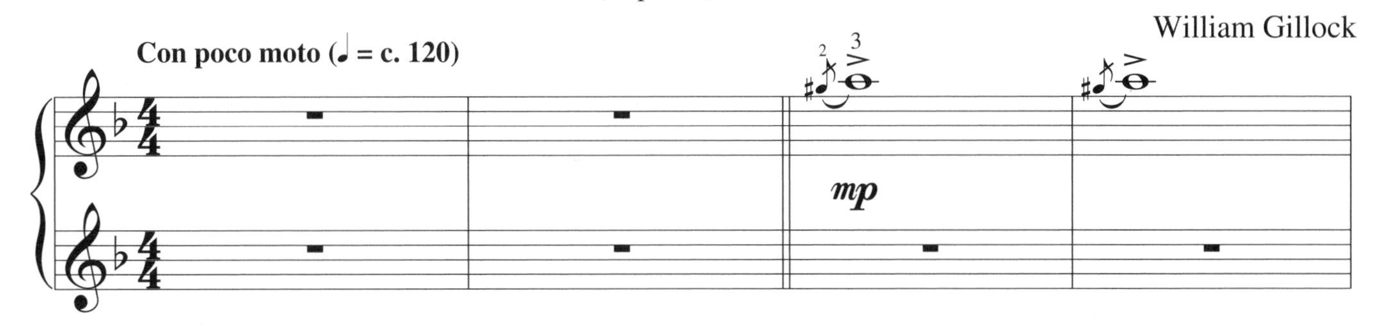

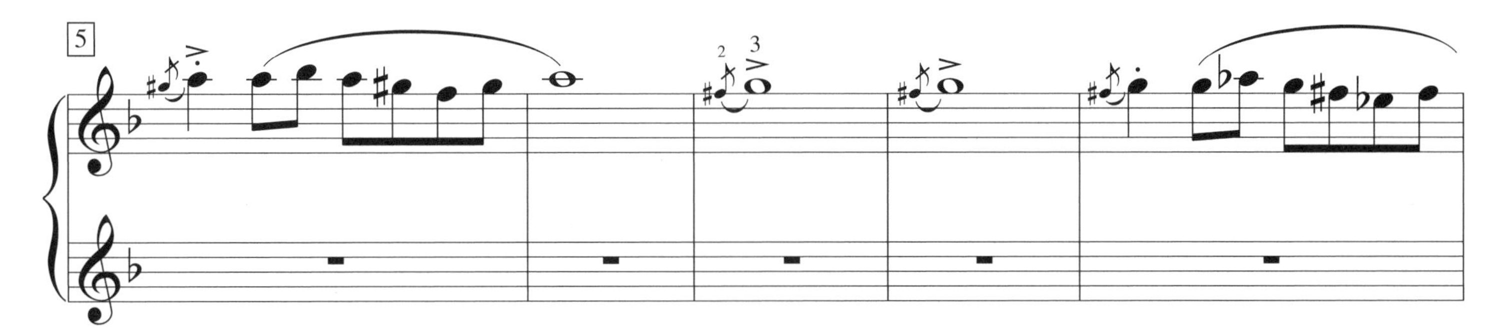

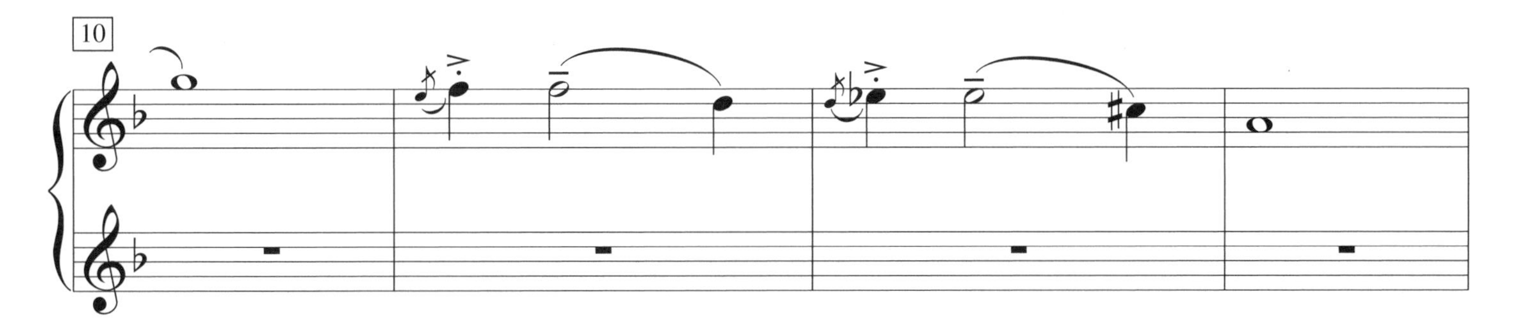

2ND PLAYER

3RD PLAYER

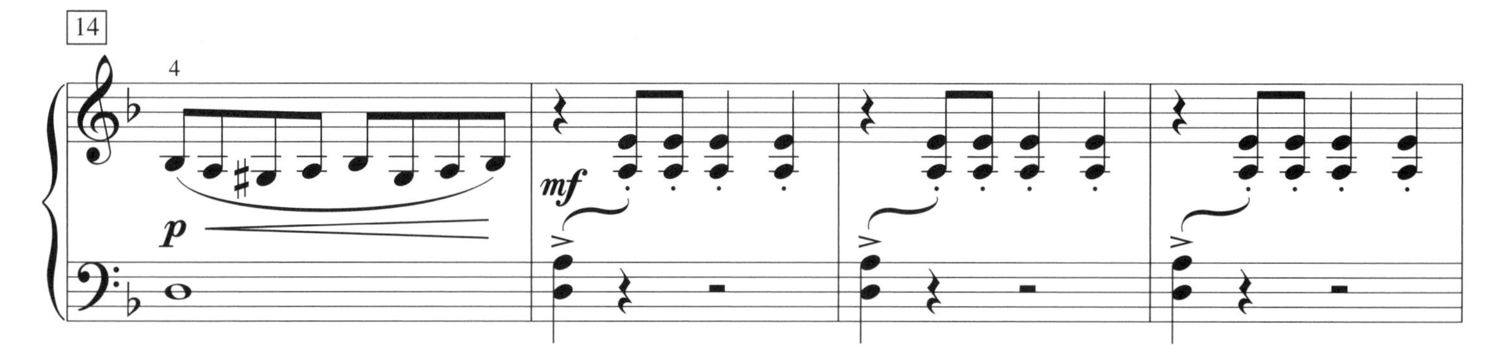

2ND PLAYER

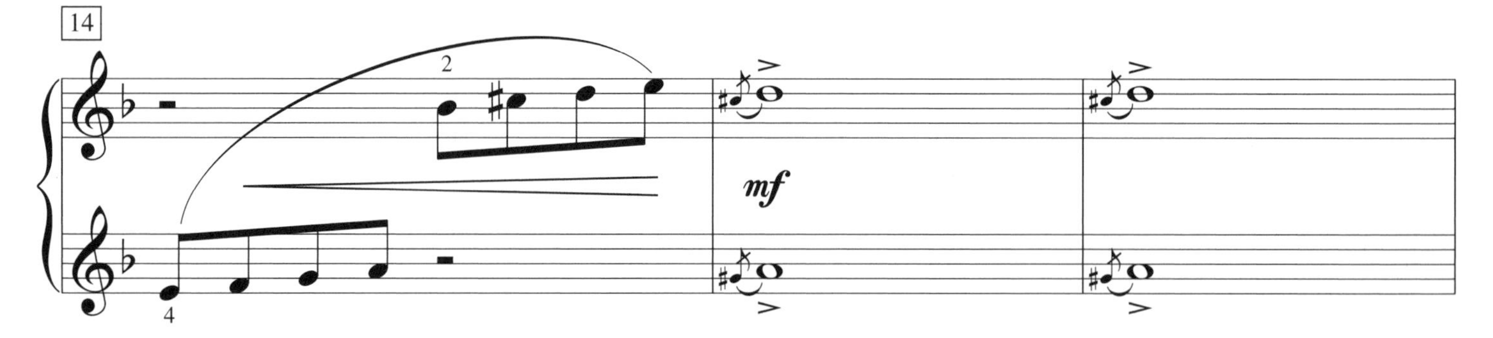

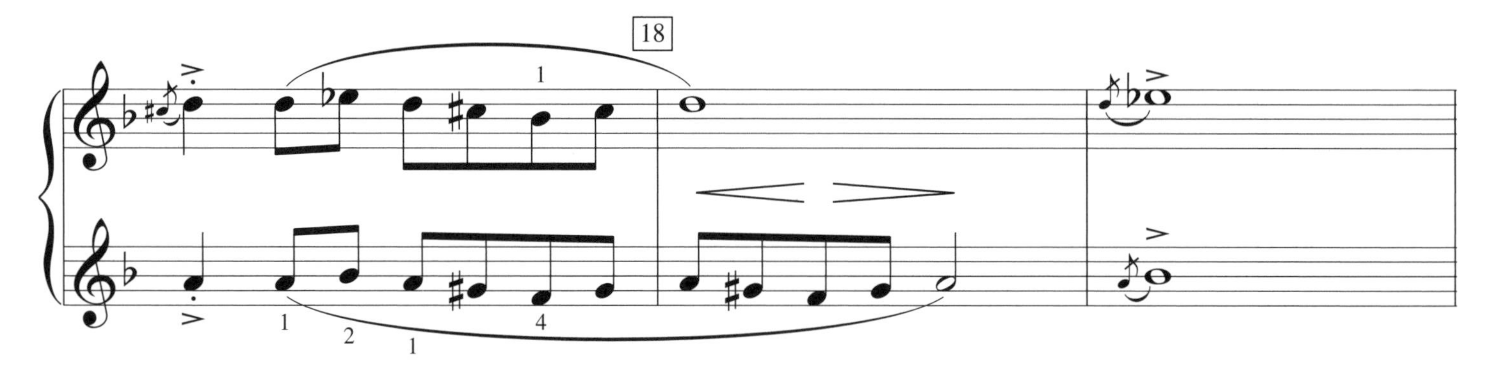

1ST PLAYER

2ND PLAYER

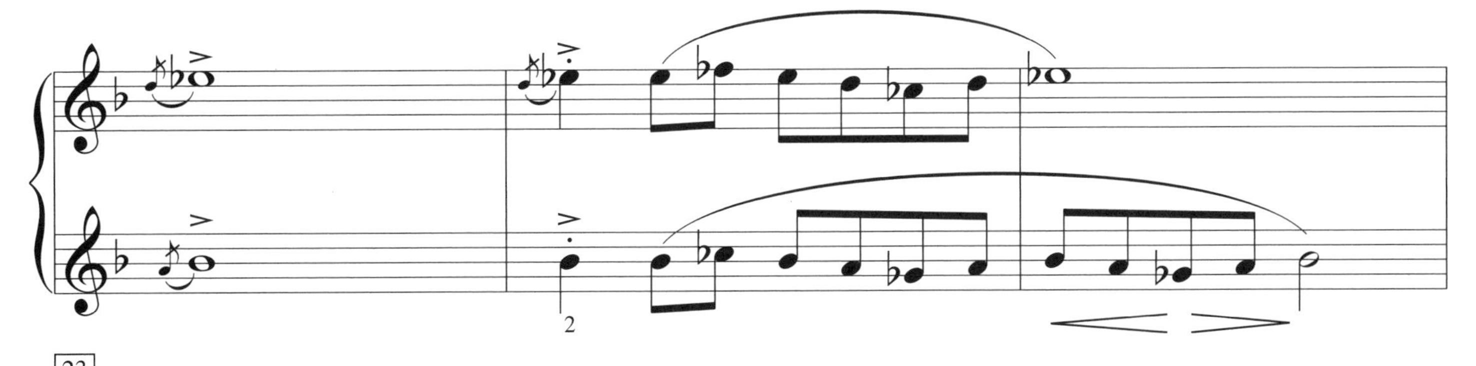

3RD PLAYER

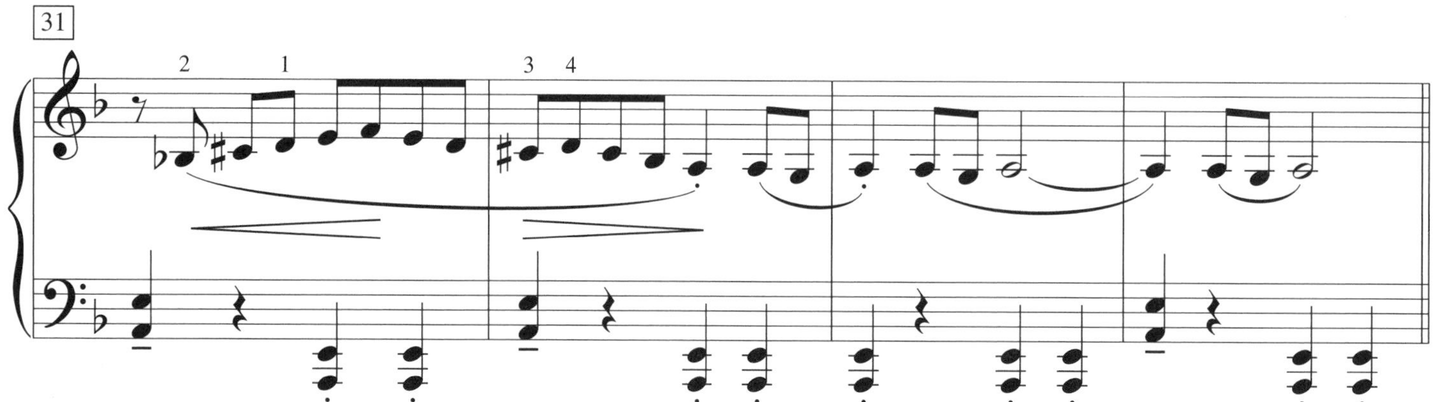

2ND PLAYER

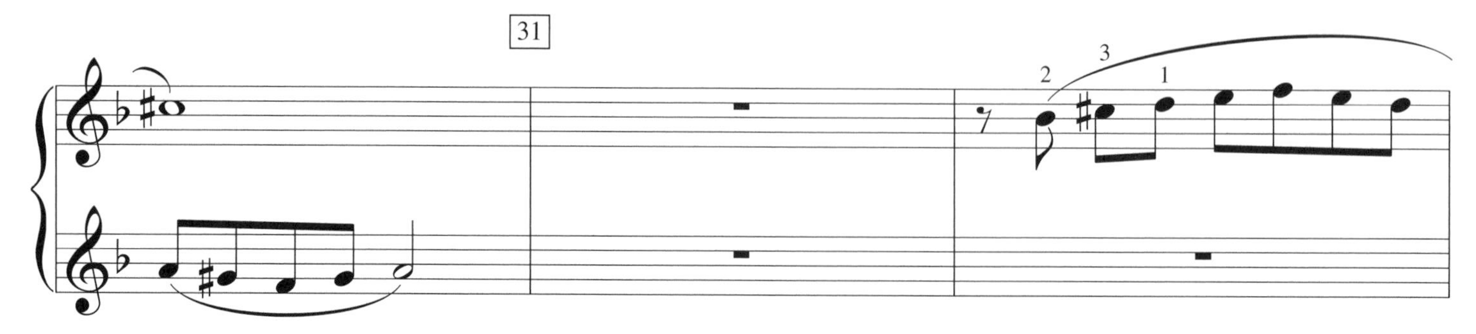

1ST PLAYER

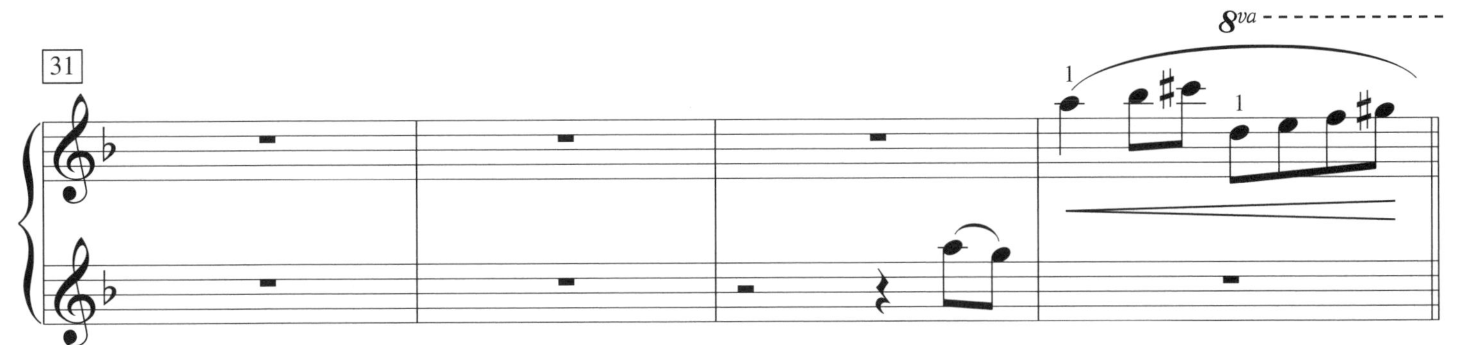

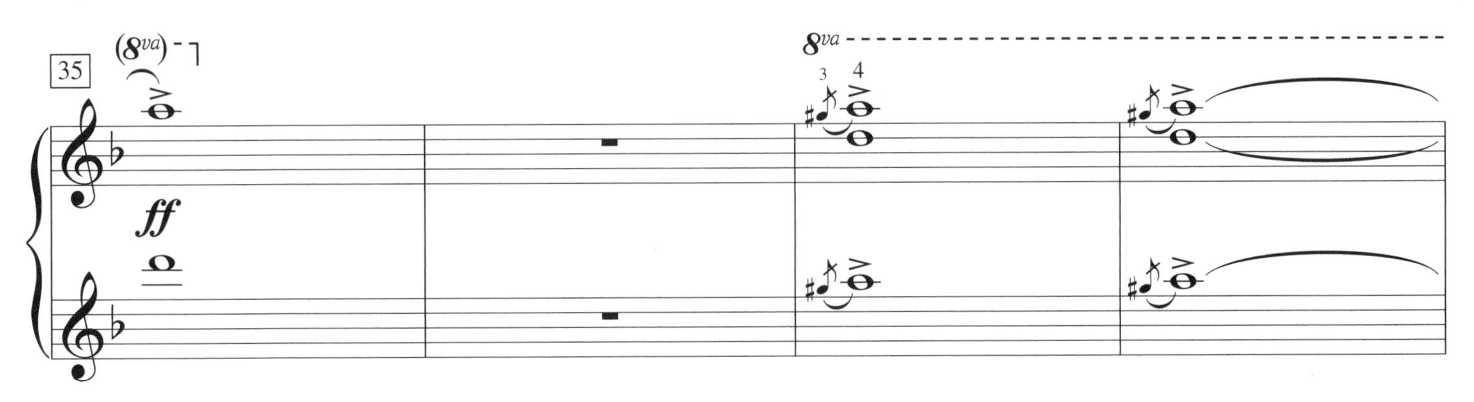

2ND PLAYER

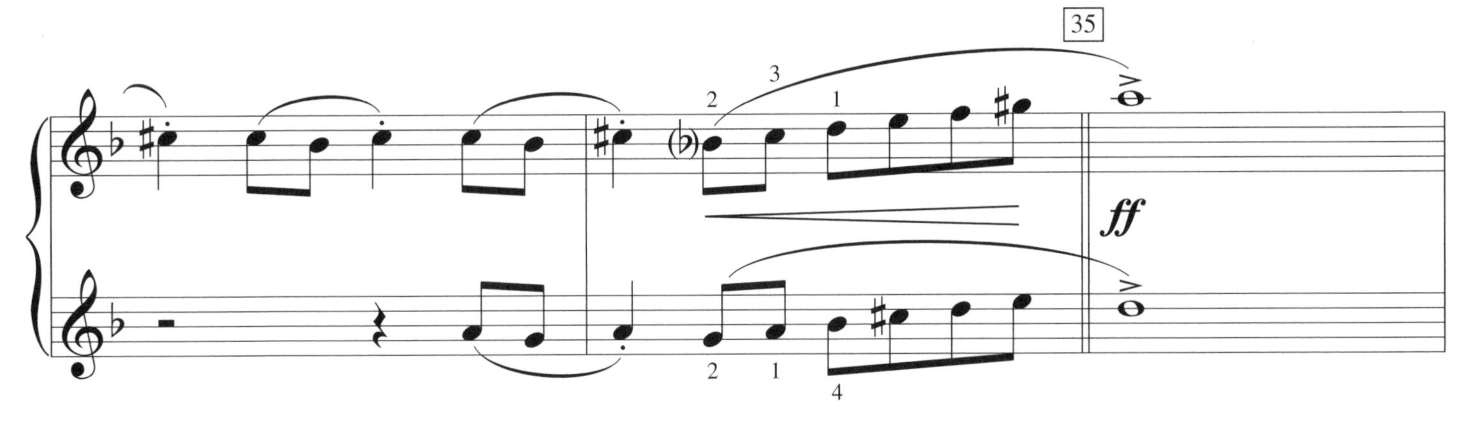

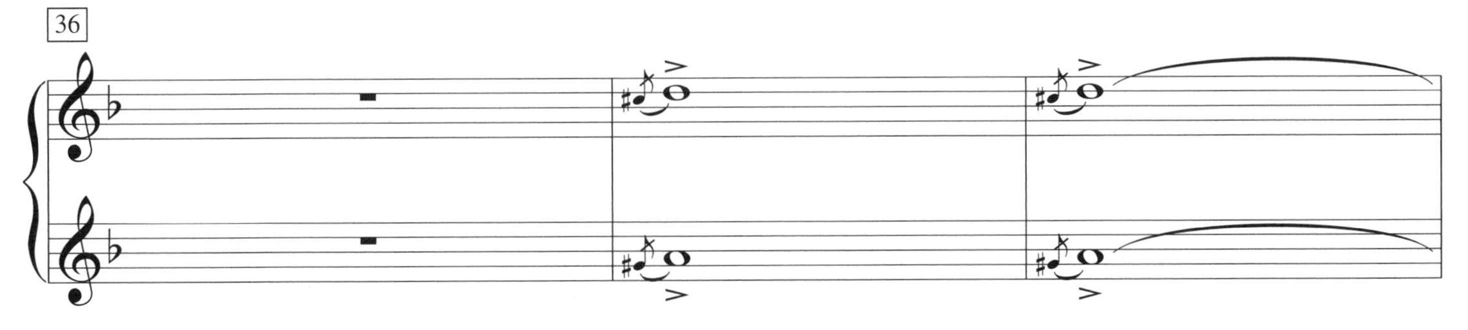

3RD PLAYER

2ND PLAYER

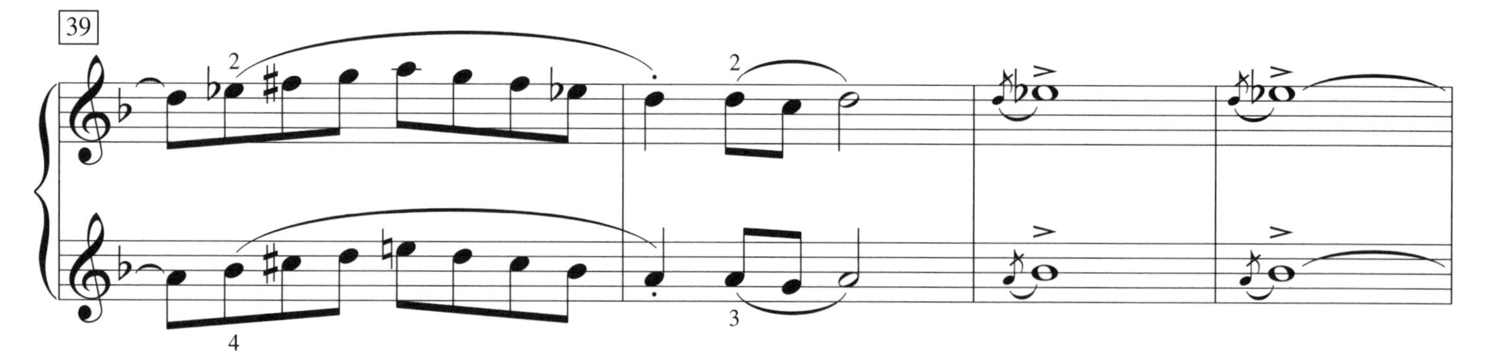

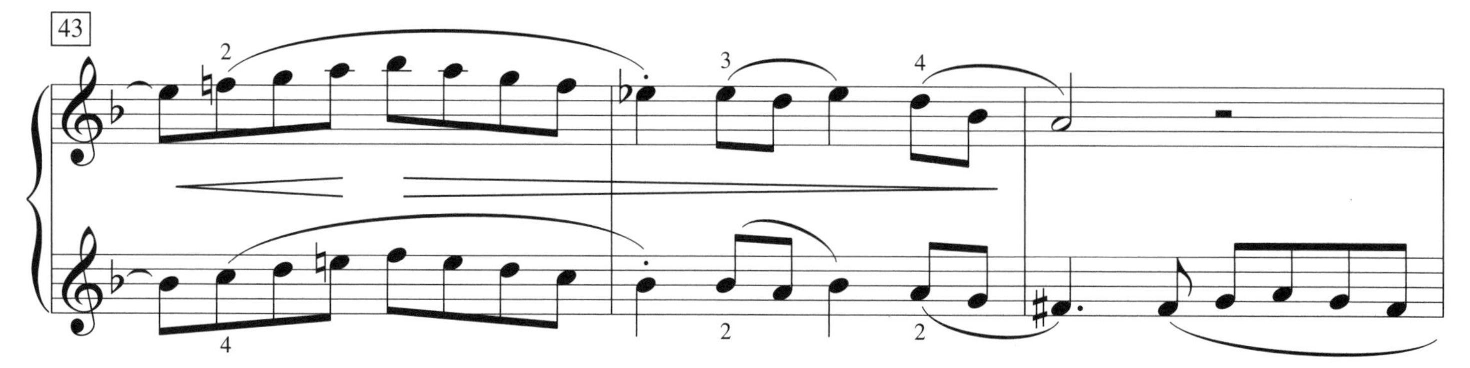

1ST PLAYER

2ND PLAYER

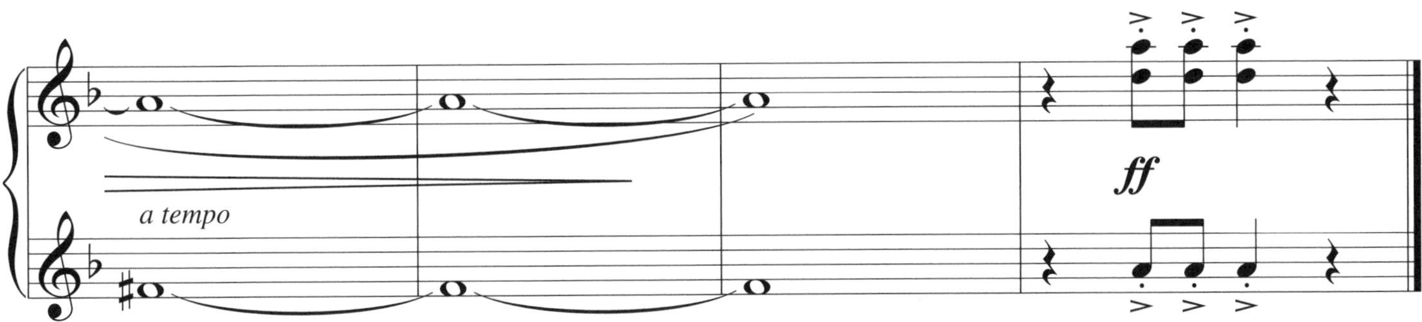

For Lauren Fine

Polka

David Karp

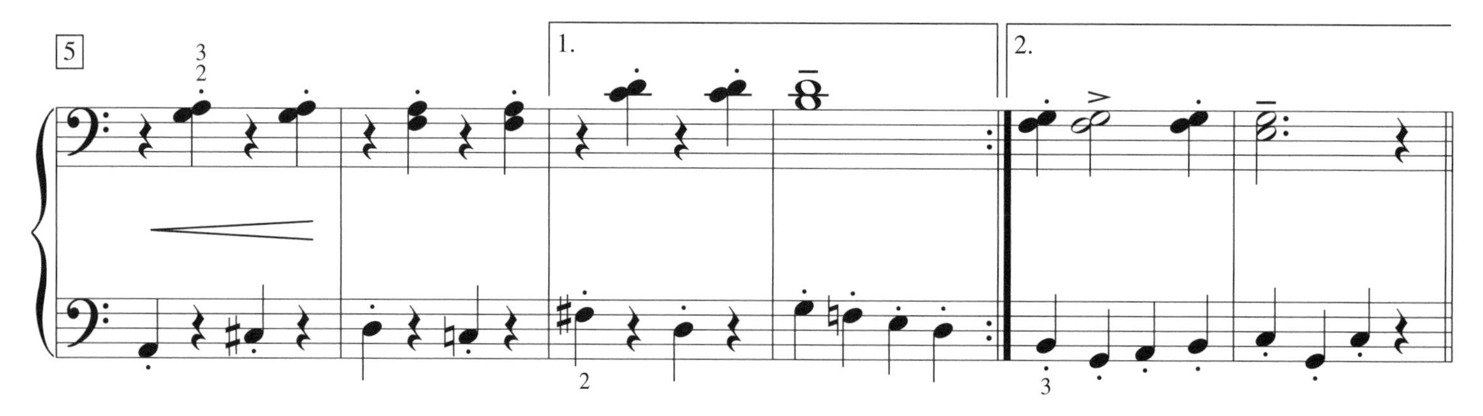

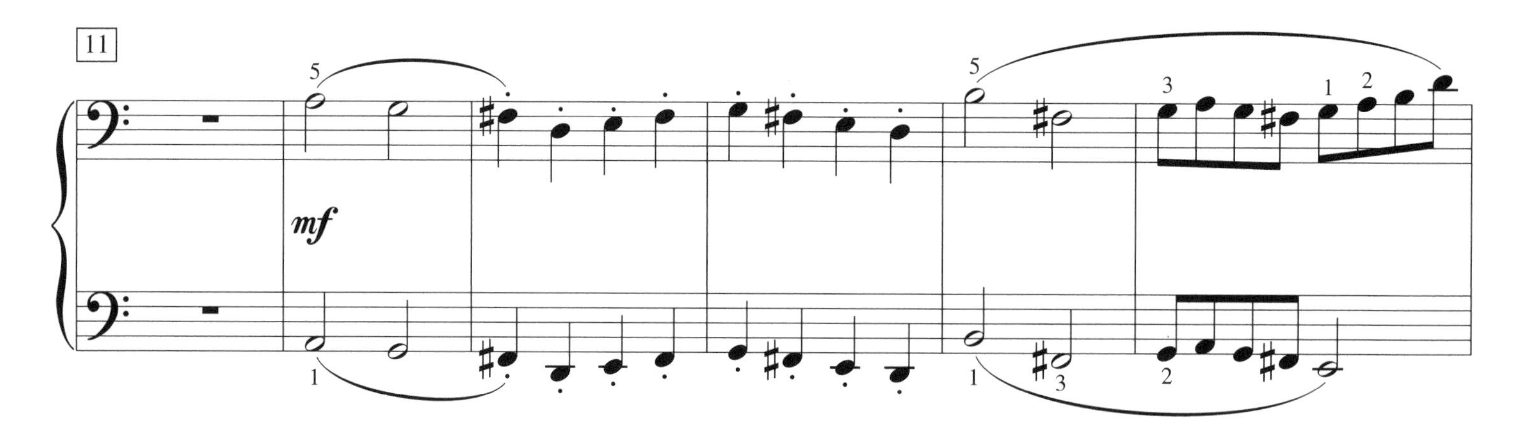

For Lauren Fine

Polka

PRIMO

David Karp

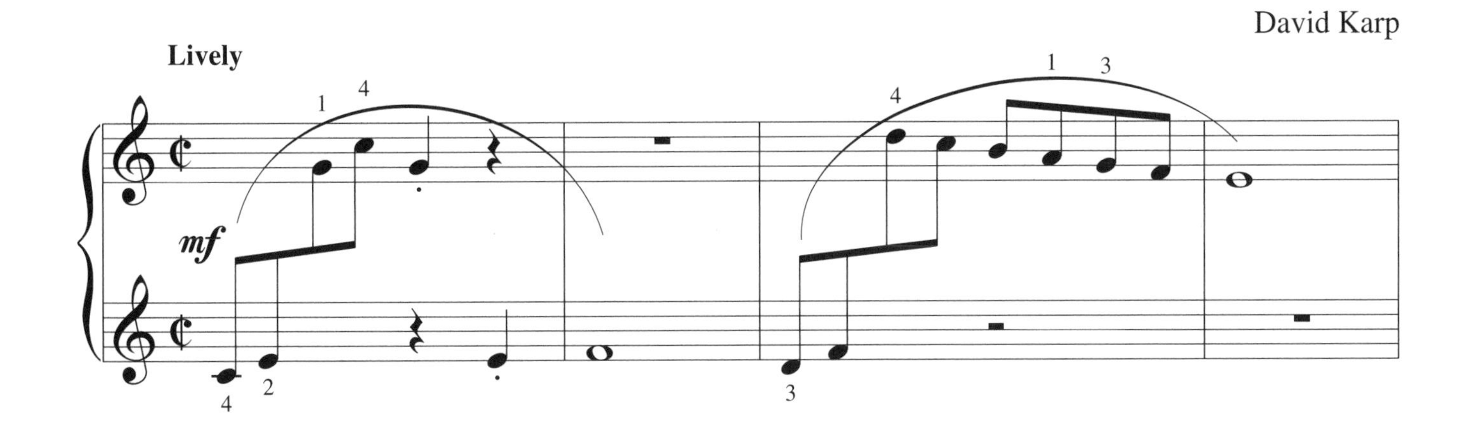

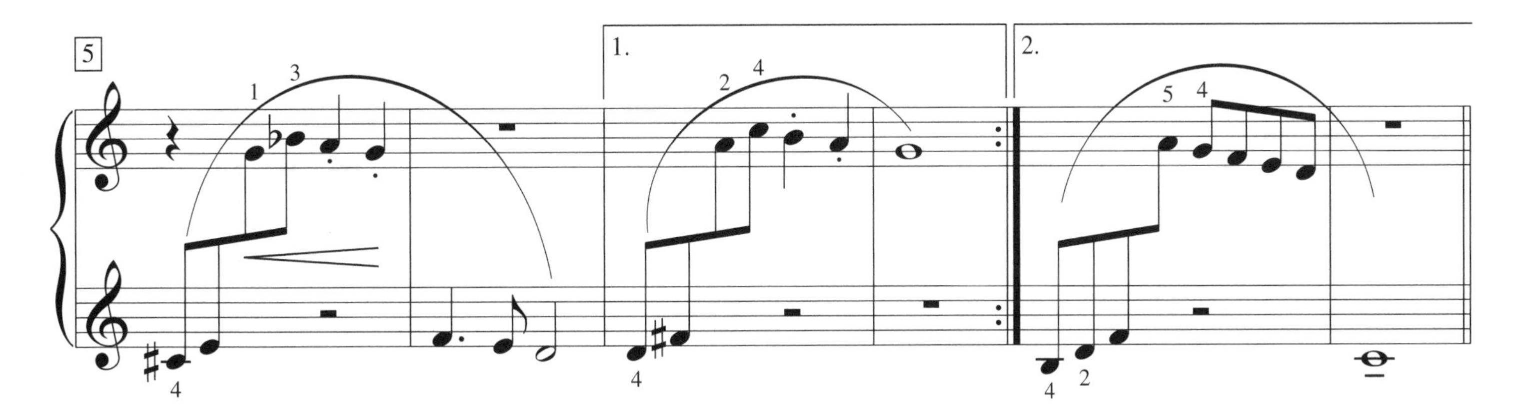

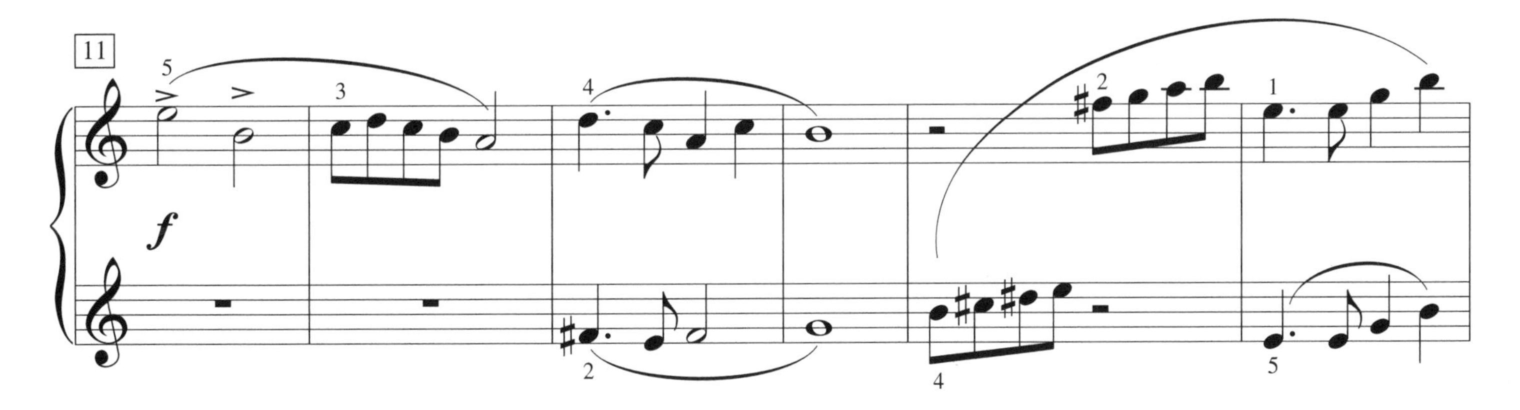

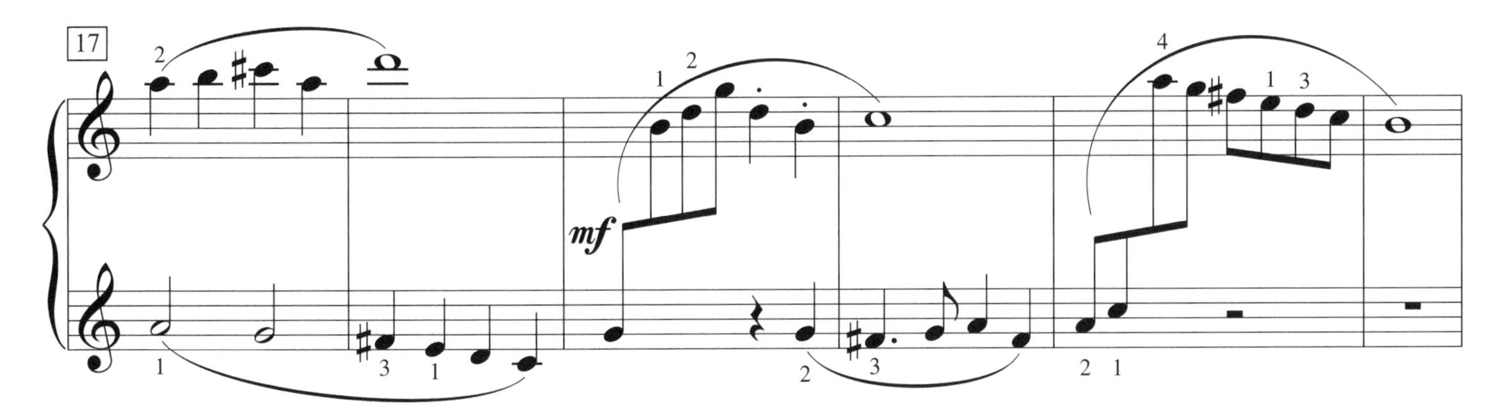

23
pp

28
cresc. poco a poco
rit.
ff

34
f a tempo

40

46

PRIMO

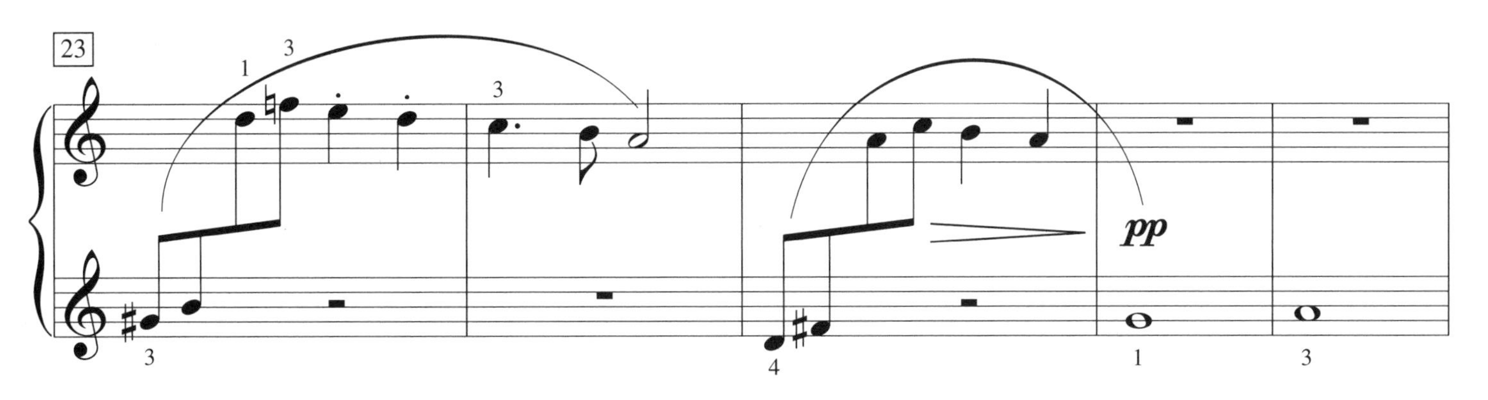

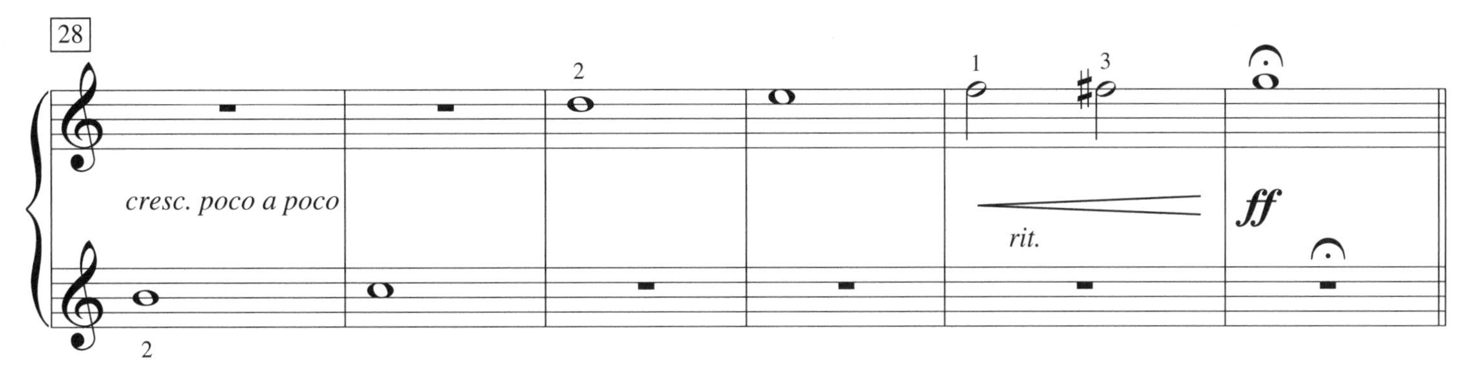

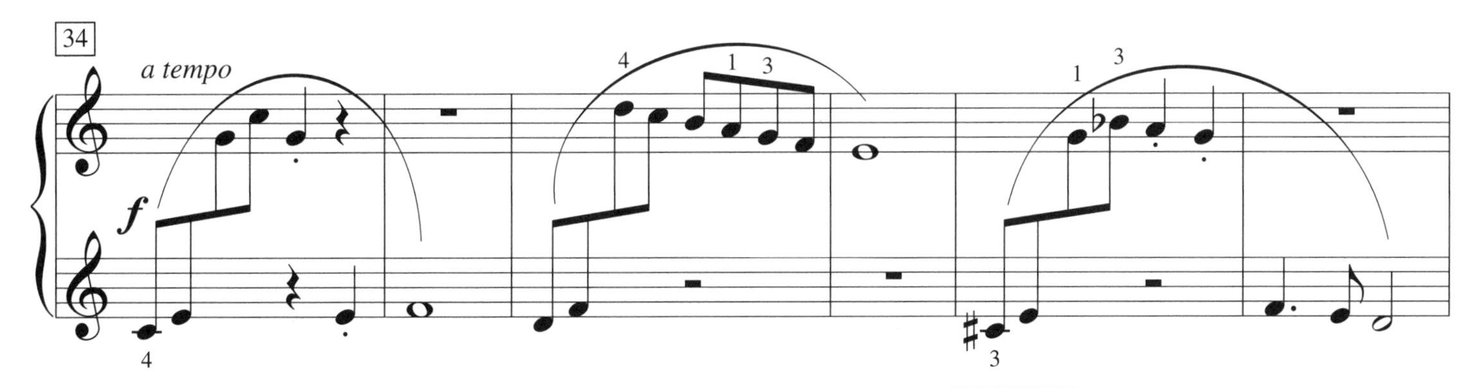

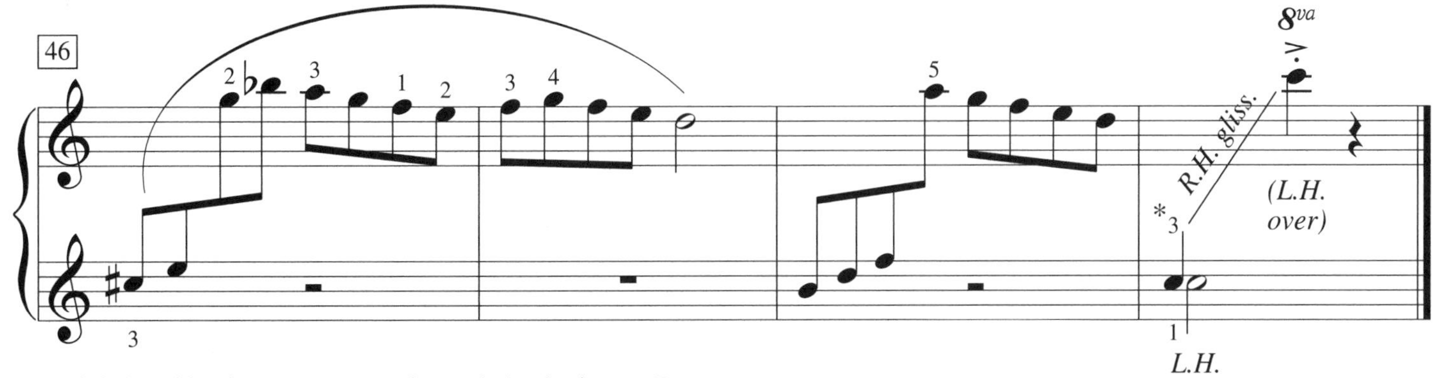

* Right hand begins two-octave *glissando* beginning on D;
Left hand crosses over to play C.

Western Bolero

SECONDO

David Karp

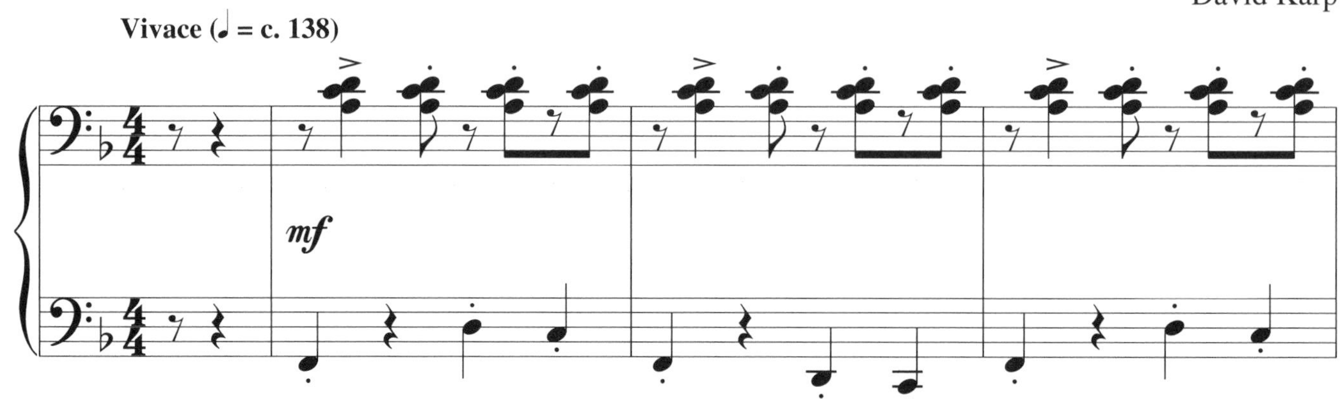

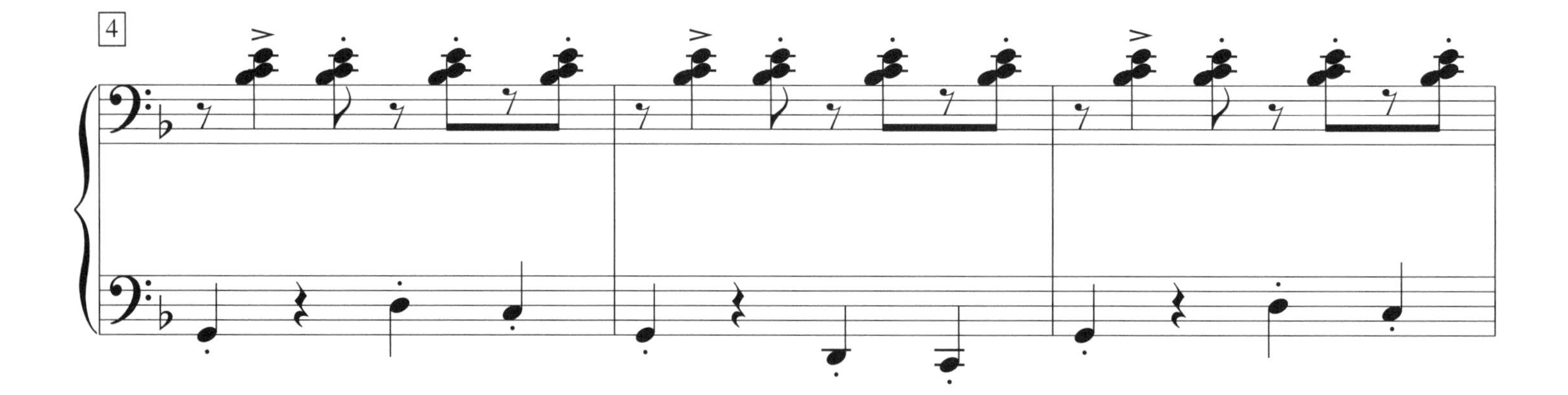

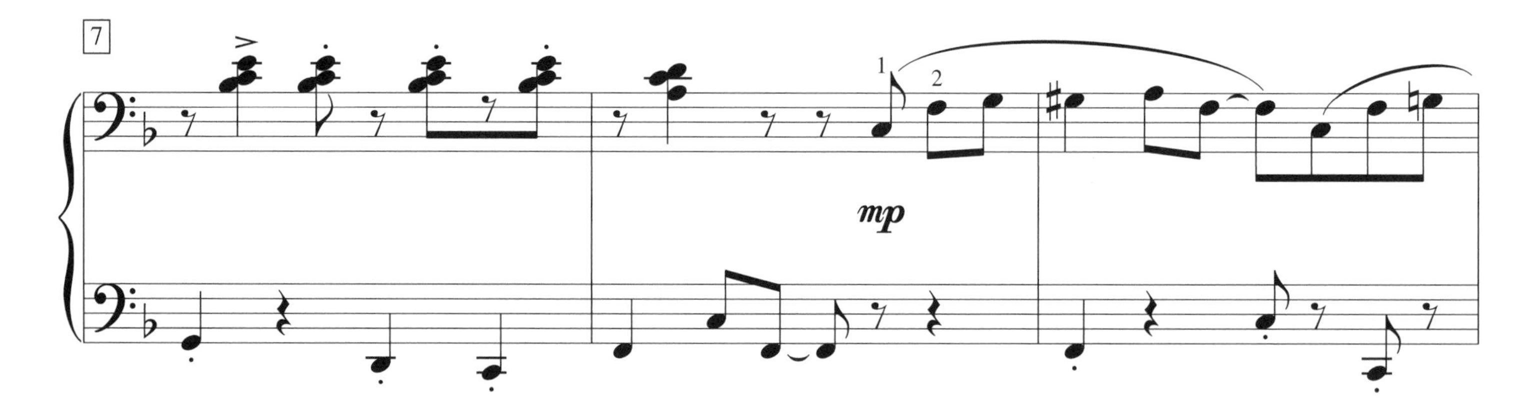

Western Bolero

PRIMO

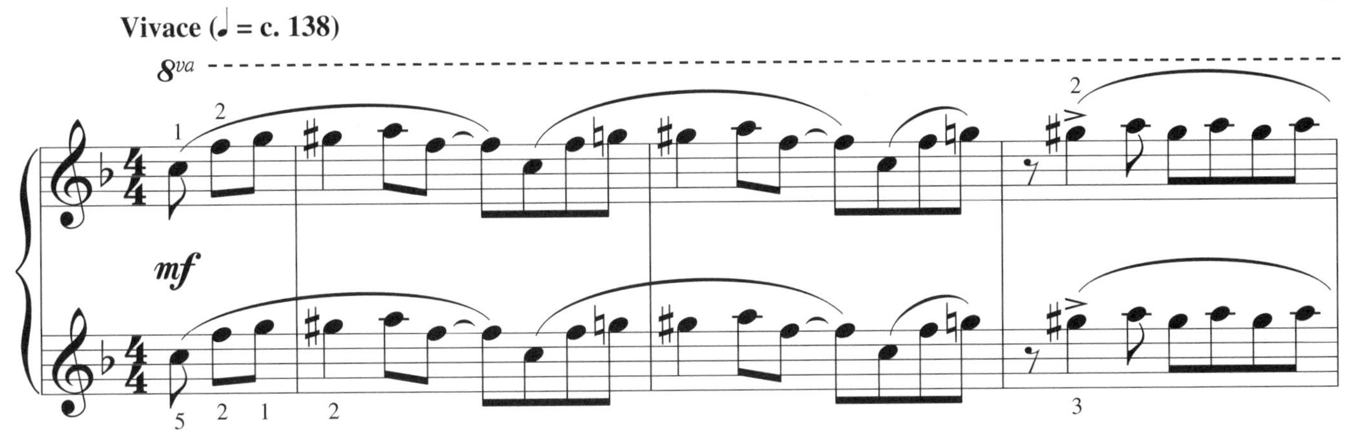

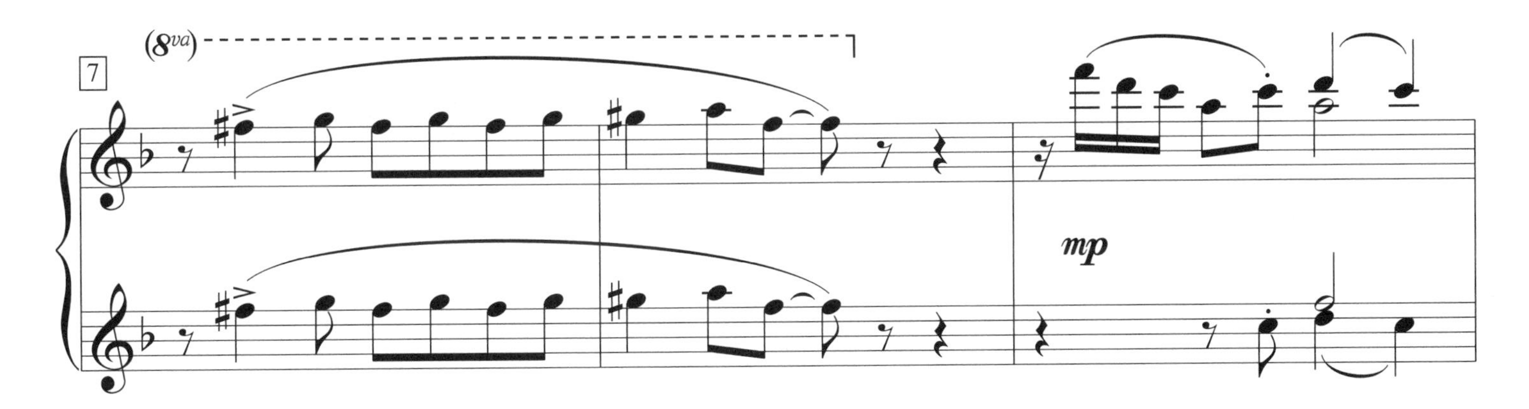

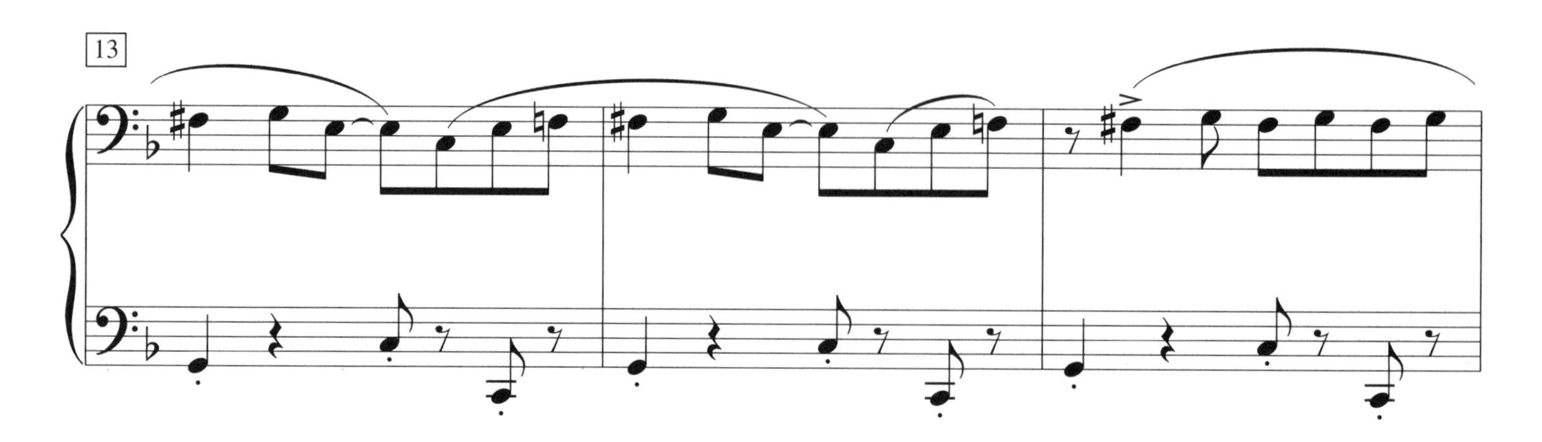
13

16

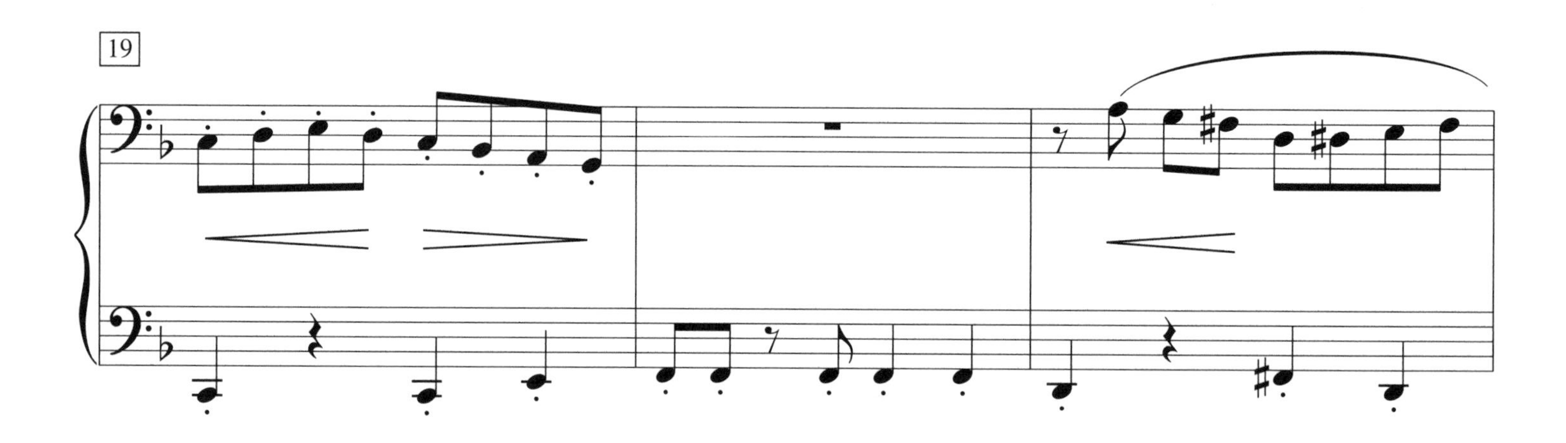
19

22

13

16
p

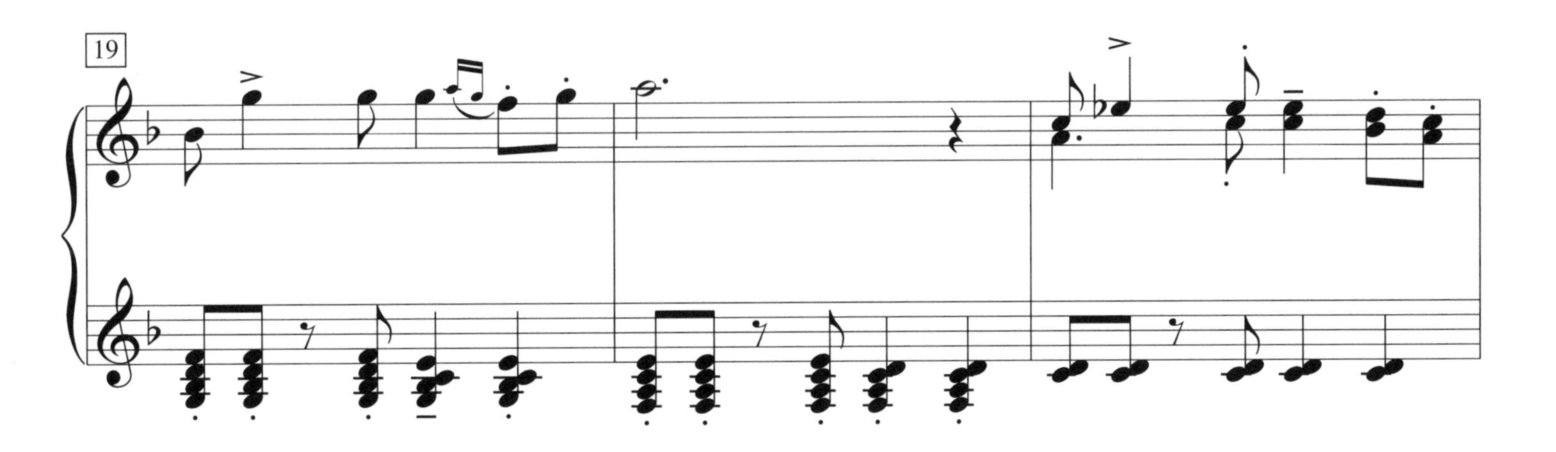
19

22
8va
mp

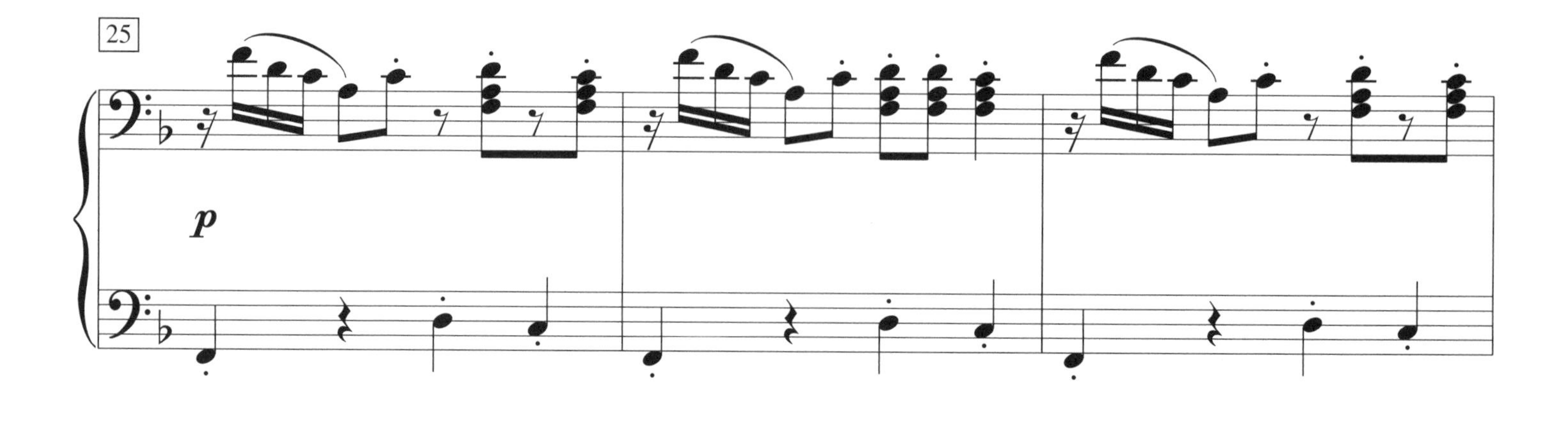
25
p

28

31

34
3
3
pp

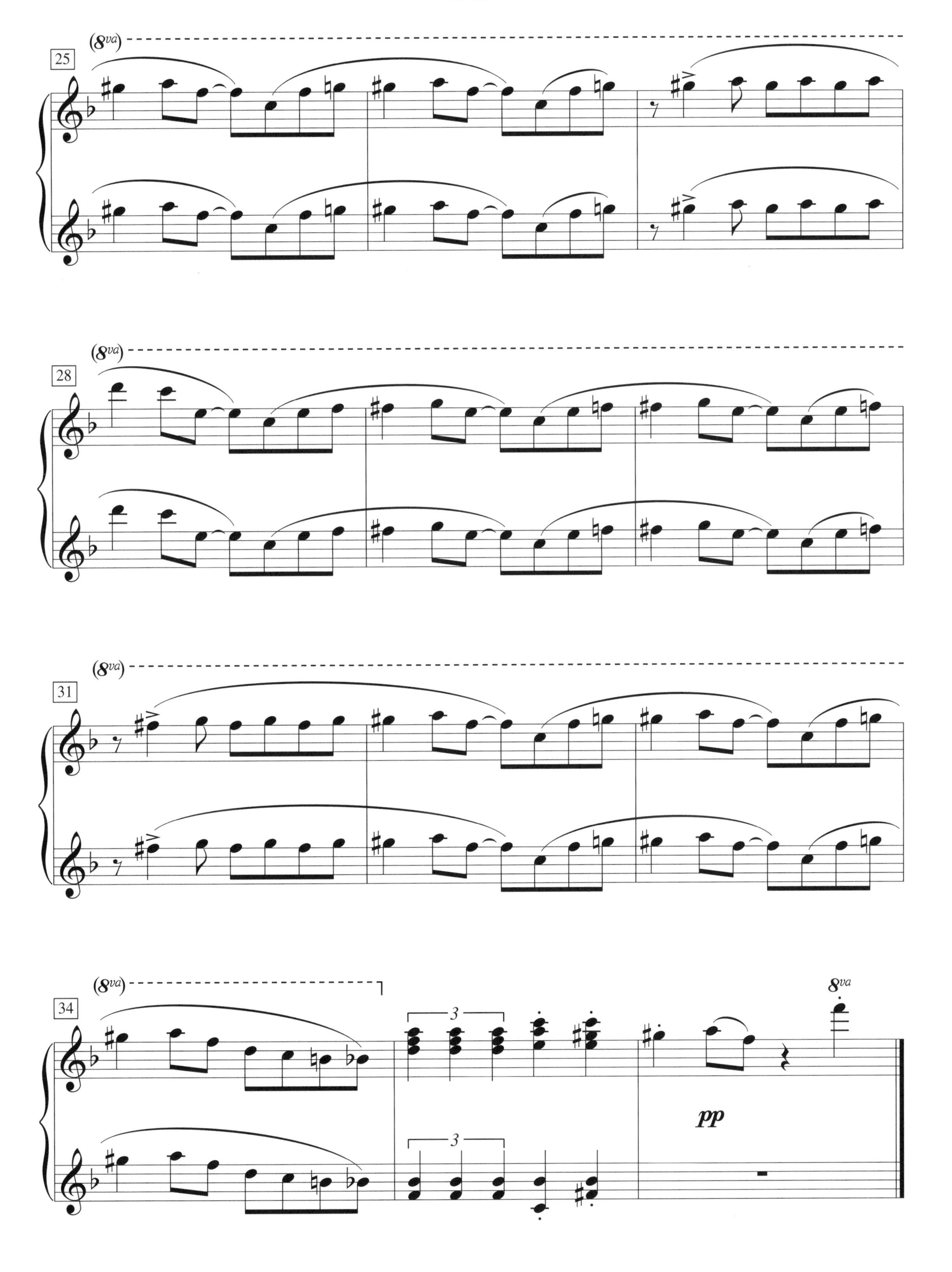
(8va)
25
28
31
34
3
8va
pp

Trepak

from *The Nutcracker Suite*

SECONDO

Peter Ilyich Tchaikovsky
Arranged by William Gillock

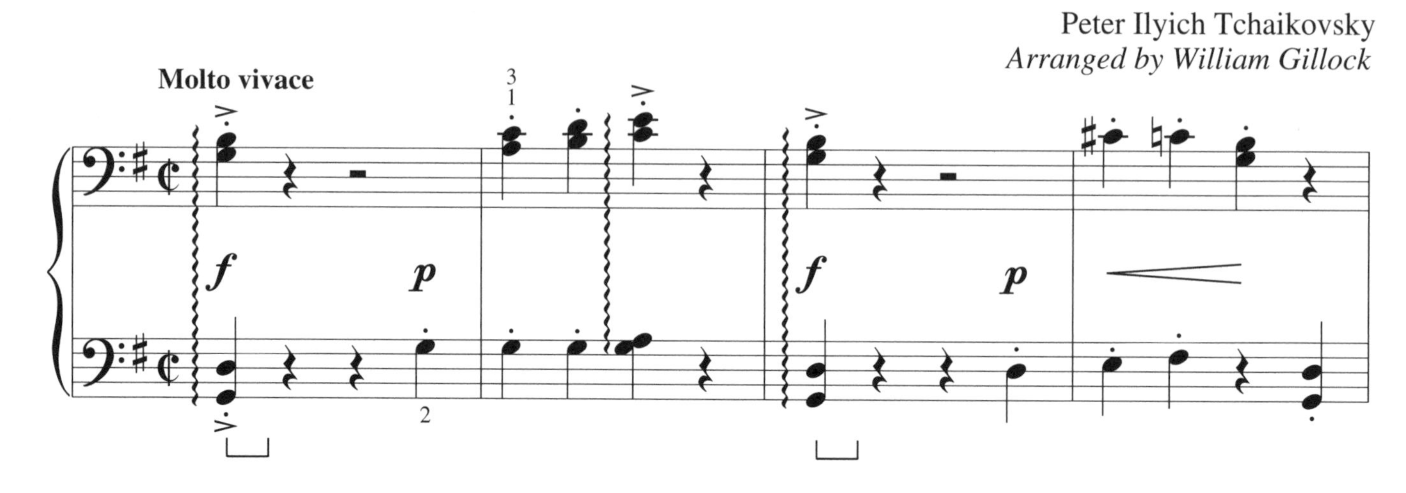

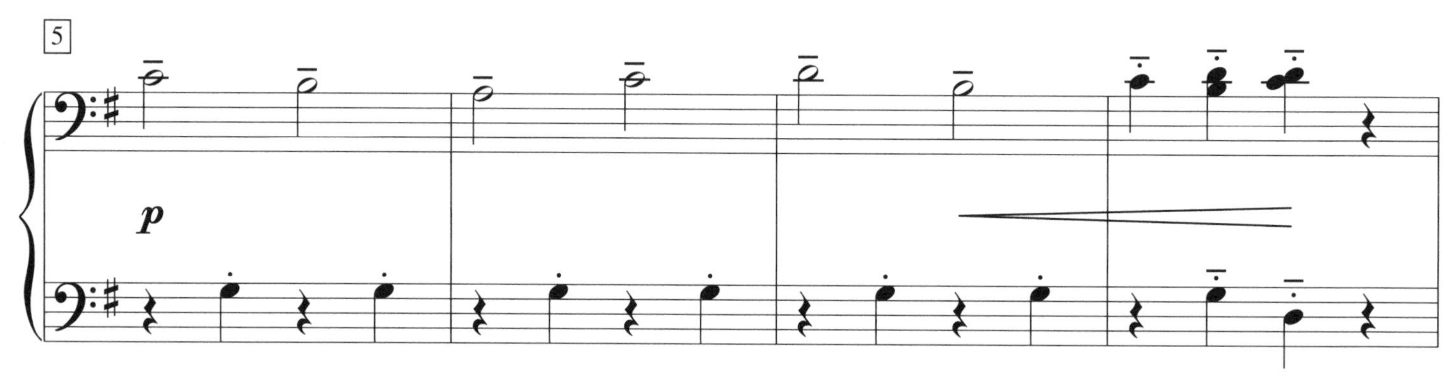

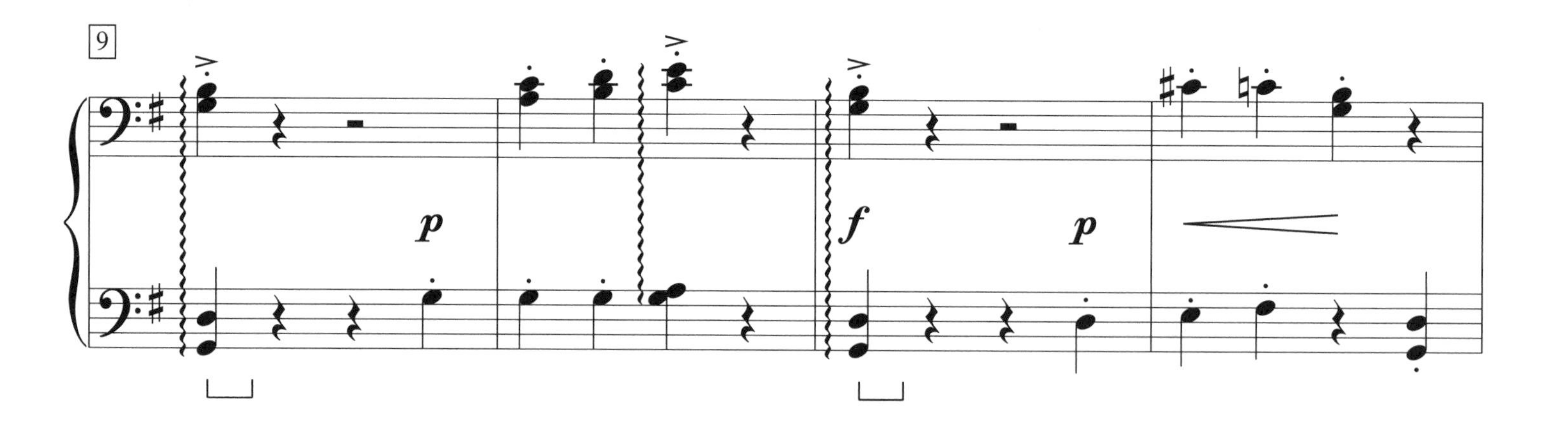

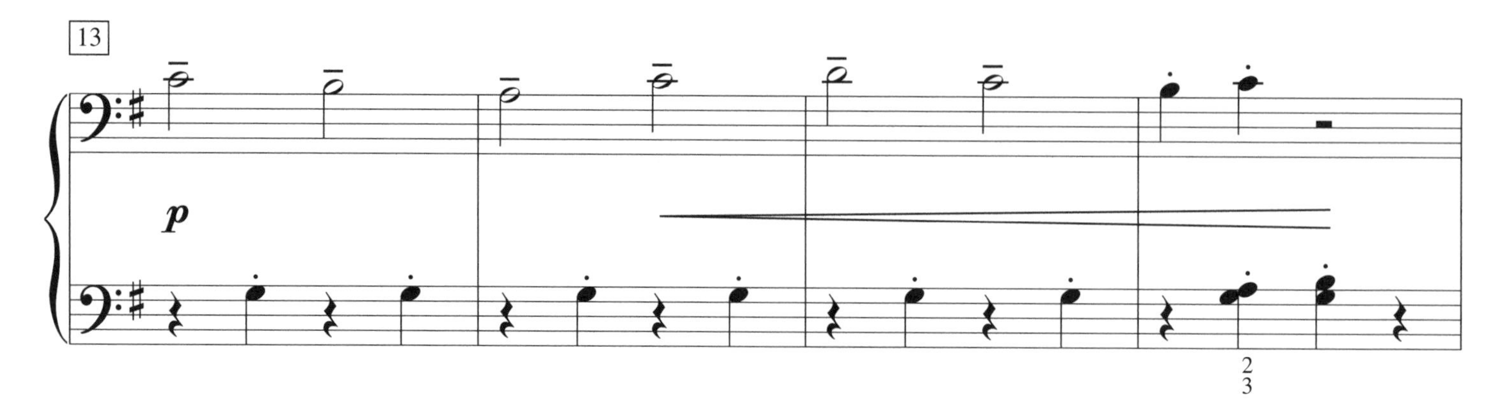

Trepak

from *The Nutcracker Suite*

PRIMO

Peter Ilyich Tchaikovsky
Arranged by William Gillock

Molto vivace

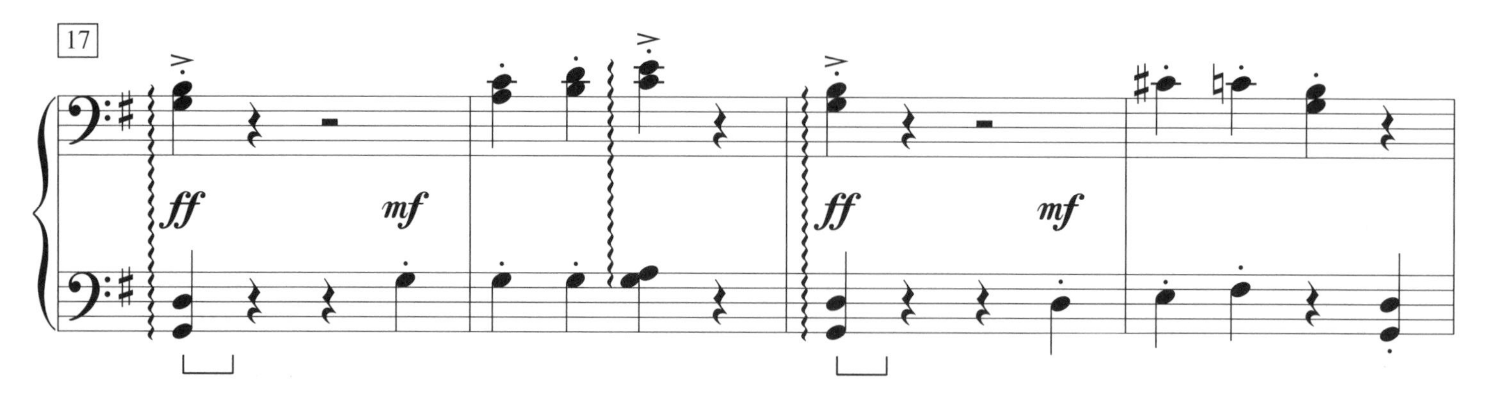
17
ff
mf
ff
mf

21
cresc.

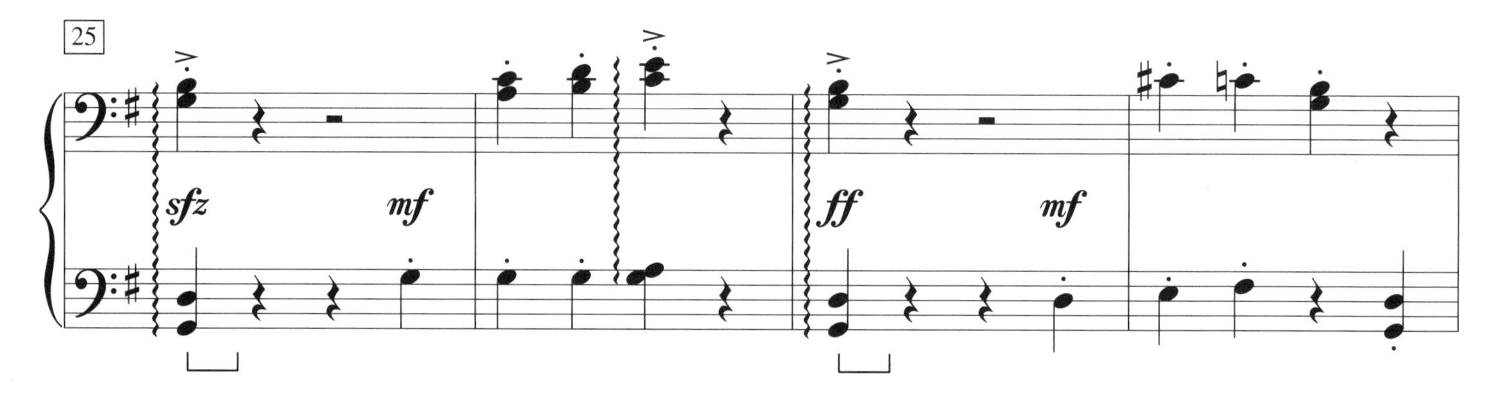
25
sfz
mf
ff
mf

29
cresc.
ff

33
mp pesante

(8va)
17
mf
ff
mf

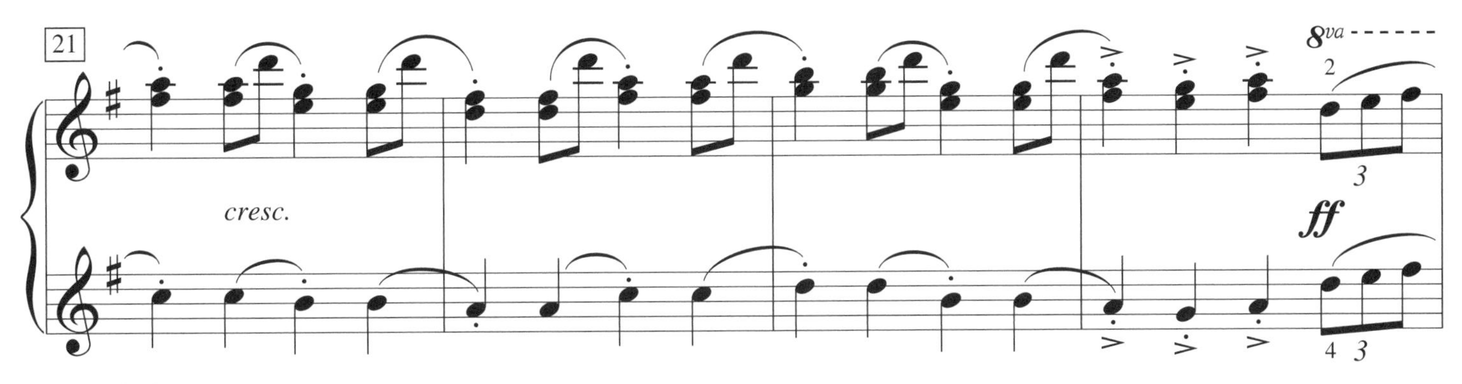
21
cresc.
8va
ff

(8va)
25
sfz
mf
ff
mf

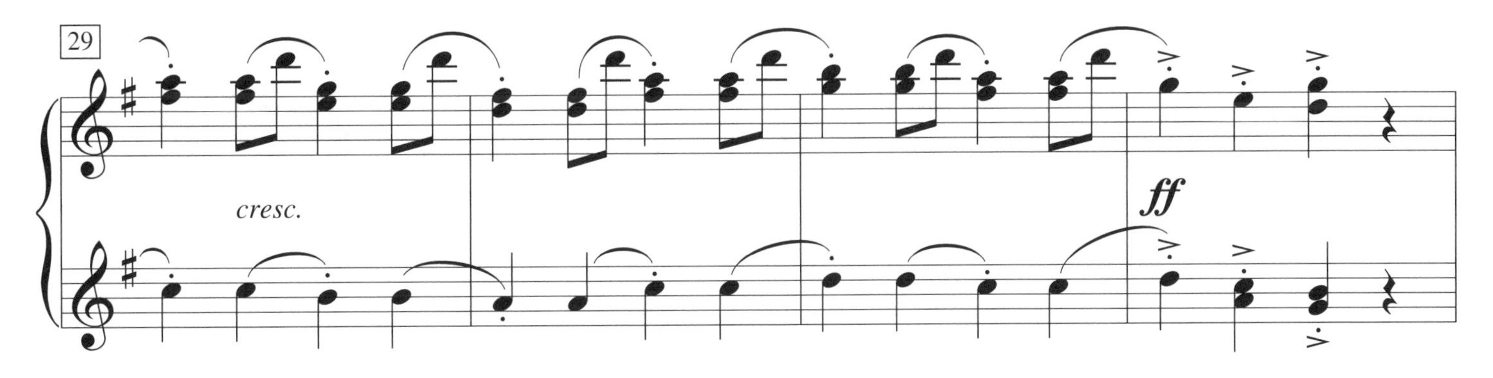
29
cresc.
ff

33
p

37
ff

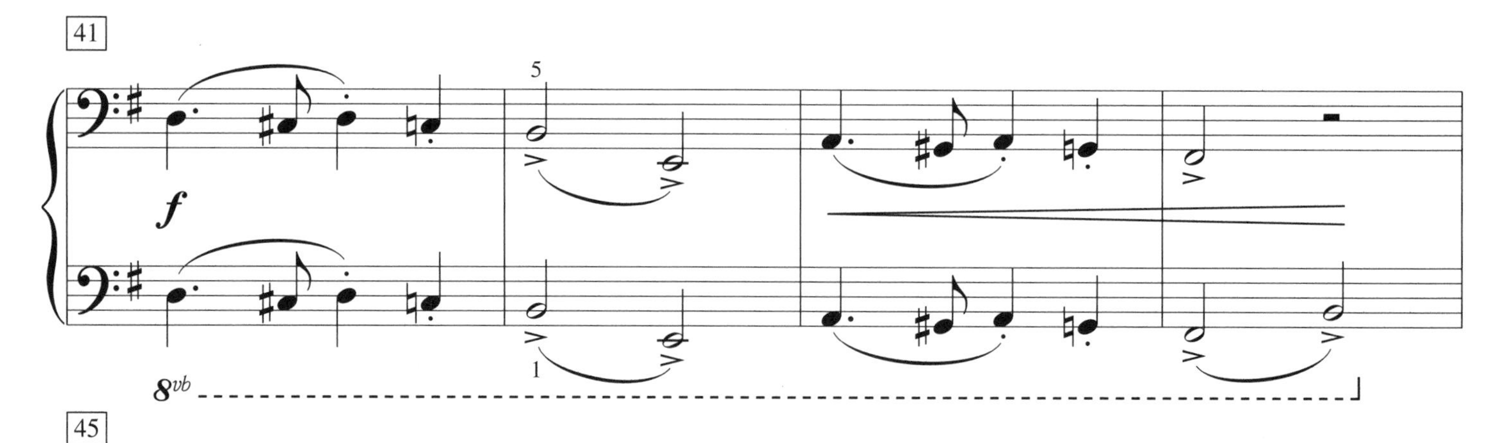
41
f
5
1
8vb

45
1
ff
5
ff

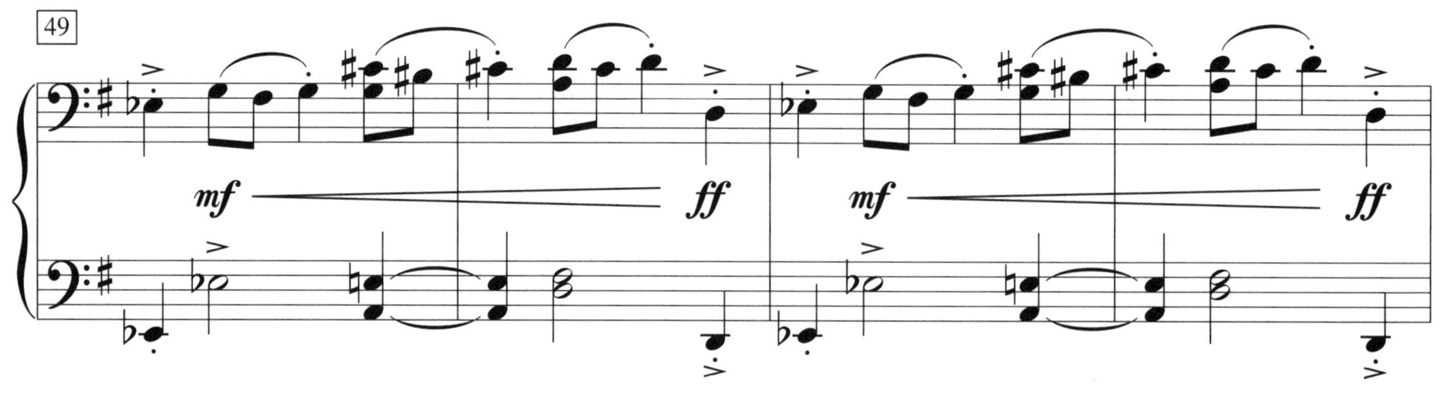
49
mf
ff
mf
ff

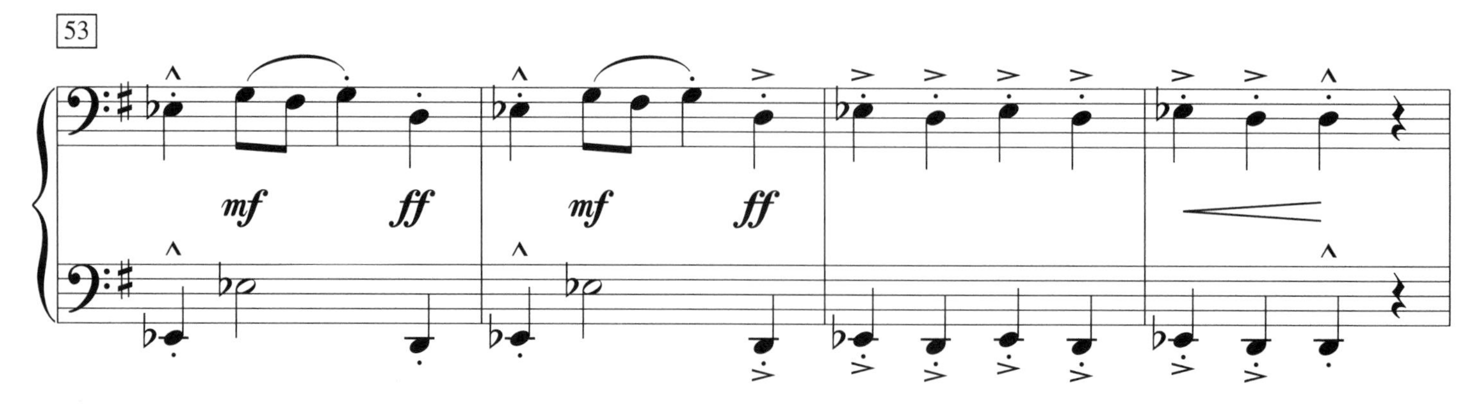
53
mf
ff
mf
ff

37
ff
marcato
41
8va
f
45
(8va)
ff
ff
49
ff
ff
53
ff
ff
fff
8va
2
3
3
4

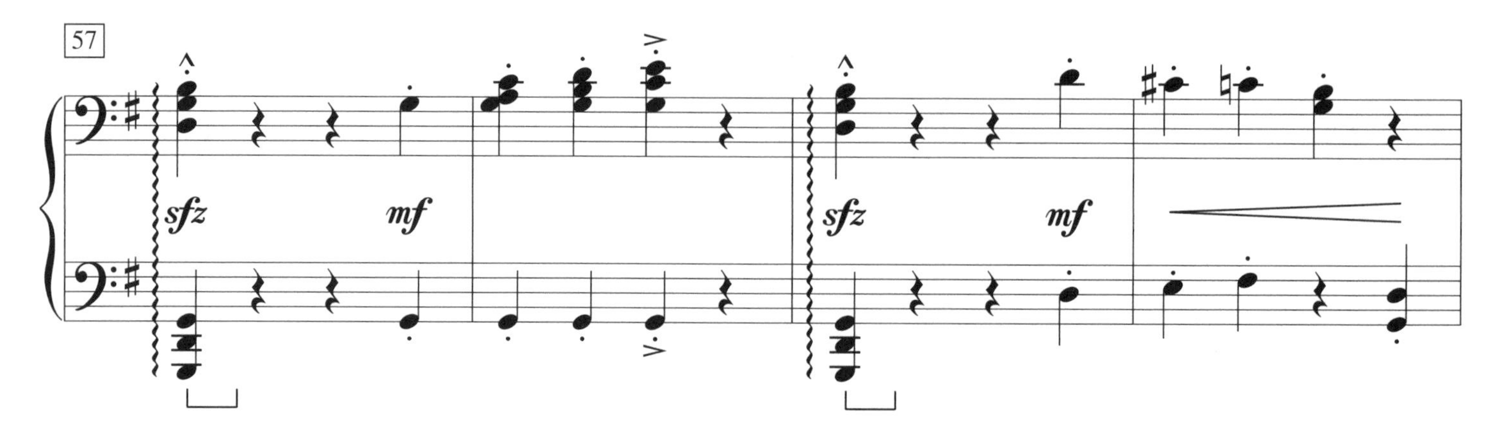
57
sfz
mf
sfz
mf

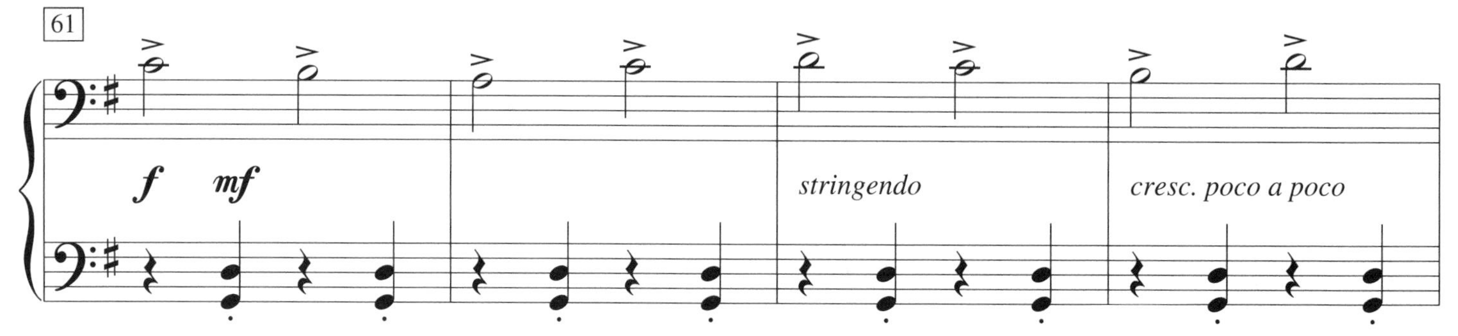
61
f
mf
stringendo
cresc. poco a poco

65

69
ff
cresc.

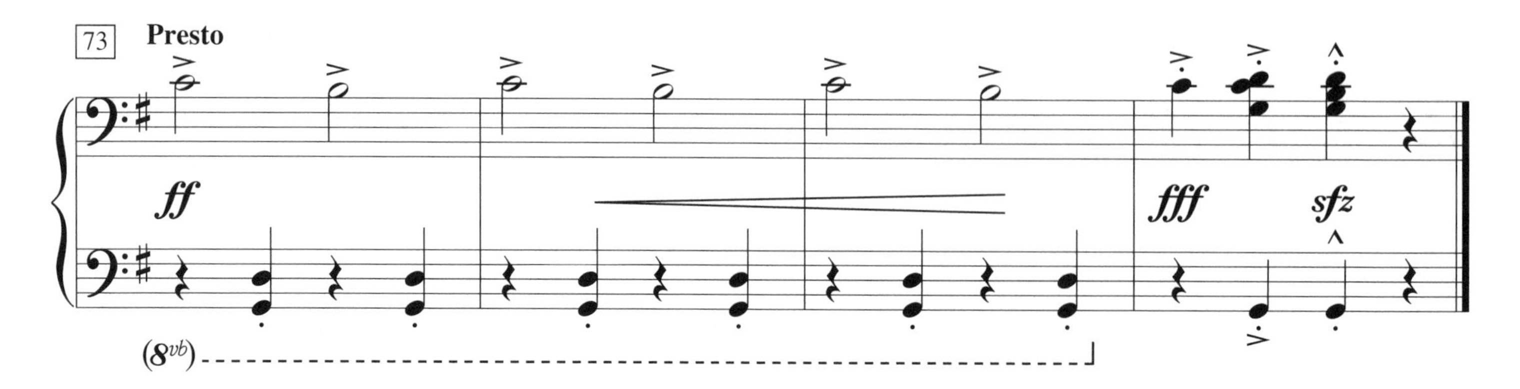
73
Presto
ff
fff
sfz

57
(8va)
sfz
mf
sfz
mf

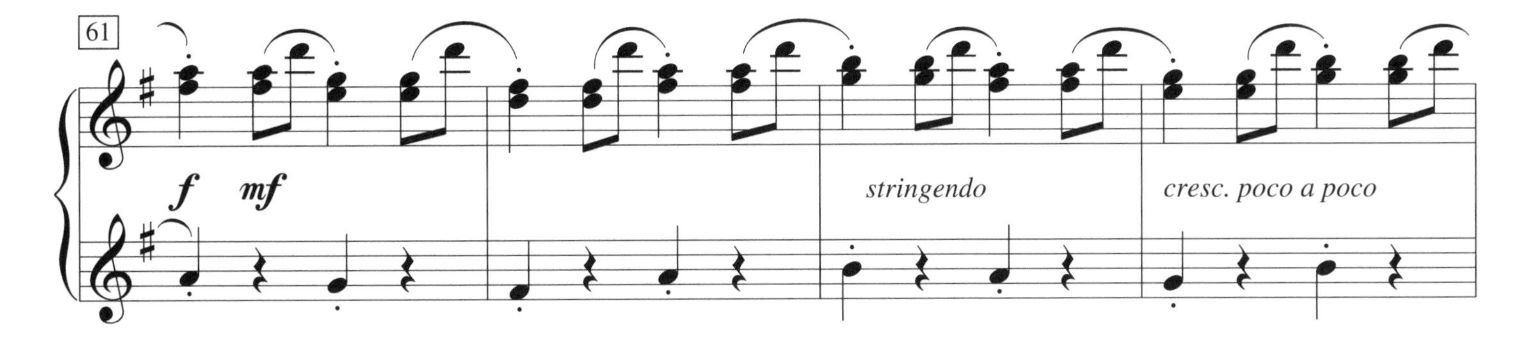
61
f
mf
stringendo
cresc. poco a poco

65

69
ff
cresc.

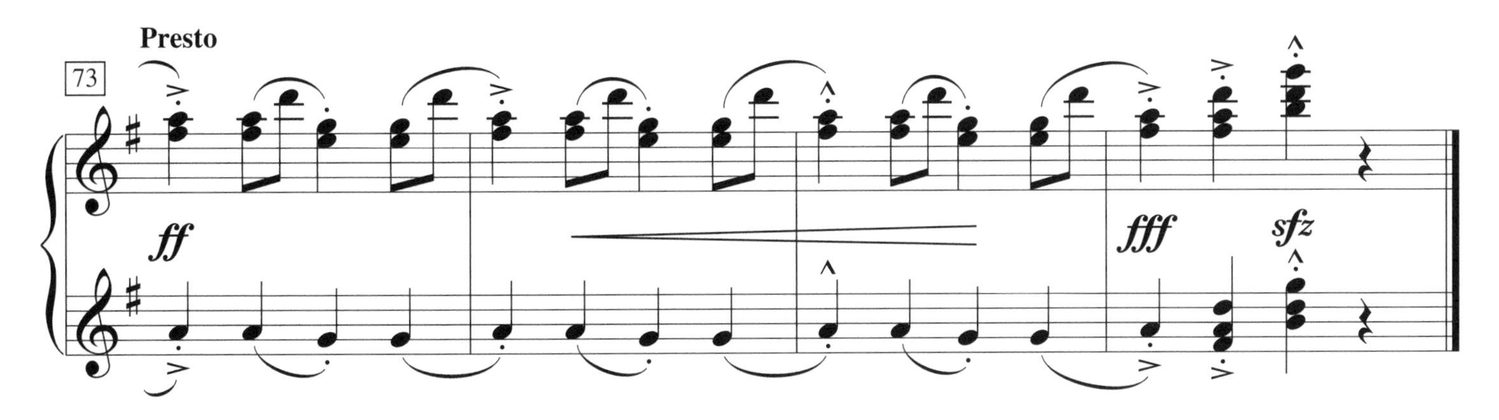
Presto
73
ff
fff
sfz

FAVORITE FESTIVAL SOLOS AND ENSEMBLES

Rediscover classic solos and duets selected by the NFMC. Each book includes up-to-date performance notes!

FAVORITE FESTIVAL SOLOS - BOOK 1

10 Great NFMC Solos

Autumn Is Here (Gillock) • Cossack Dance (Gillock) • Fiesta Fun (Miller) • Indian Dance (Miller) • A New Day (Setliff) • Punch and Judy (Baumgartner) • The Python (Hartsell) • Stately Procession (Gillock) • The Whiskery Walrus (Austin) • Wind in the Bamboo Tree (Gillock).

00416930 .... $7.99

FAVORITE FESTIVAL SOLOS - BOOK 2

10 Great NFMC Solos

Black Cat Bounce (Austin) • Dance in E Minor (Miller) • Evening Lament (Hartsell) • Fountain Square (Baumgartner) • Going Baroque (Austin) • Little Waltz (Miller) • On the Champs-Elysees (Gillock) • Rondo in Classic Style (Gillock) • Whirlwind (Baumgartner) • Wistful Chant (Peskanov).

00119162 .... $7.99

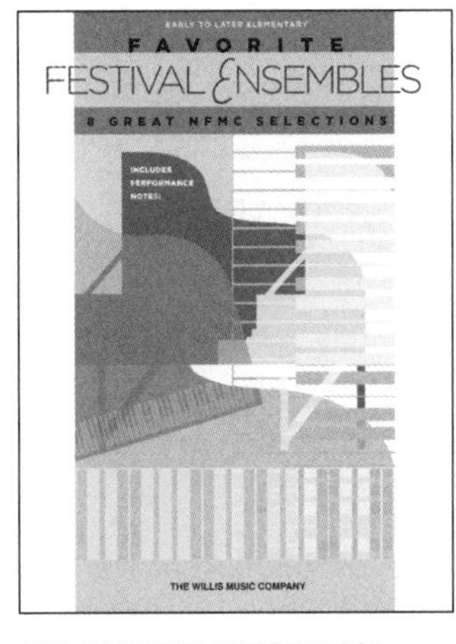

FAVORITE FESTIVAL ENSEMBLES - BOOK 1

8 Great NFMC Duets and Trios

Chiapanecas (arr. Burnam) • March of the Jumping Jacks (Bilbro) • The Old-Time Fiddler (Gaynor-Blake) • On the Trail (Miller) • Peace Pipe (Karp) • Rock-a-bye Five (Hall) • Song Without Words (Karp) • The Star-Spangled Banner (arr. Nevin).

00416931 .... $7.99

FAVORITE FESTIVAL ENSEMBLES - BOOK 2

8 Great NFMC Duets and Trios

The Chase (Miller/Engle) • Kibbutz Capers (Karp) • Oriental Bazaar (Gillock) • Petite Spanish Dance (Miller) • Pinwheels (Beard) • Polka (Karp) • Trepak (Tchaikovsky/Gillock) • Western Bolero (Karp).

00119195 ....$8.99

Prices, content, and availability subject to change without notice.

www.willispianomusic.com **www.facebook.com/willispianomusic**

Dynamic Duets

and Exciting Ensembles from Willis Music!

SELECTED COLLECTIONS

00416804 Accent on Duets (MI-LI) / *William Gillock*..........$12.99

00416822 All-American Ragtime Duets (EI) / *Glenda Austin* $7.99

00416732 Concerto No. 1 for Piano and Strings (MI) (2P, 4H) / *Alexander Peskanov* $14.95

00416898 Duets in Color Book 1 (EI-MI) / *Naoko Ikeda* $12.99

00406230 First Piano Duets (EE) / *John Thompson* series $4.95

00416805 New Orleans Jazz Styles Duets (EI) / *Gillock, arr. Austin*..........$9.99

00416830 Teaching Little Fingers Easy Duets (EE) / *arr. Miller* $5.99

SELECTED SHEETS

Early Elementary

00406709 Flying (1P, 4H) / *Carolyn Miller*.. $2.50

00406743 Wisteria (1P, 4H) / *Carolyn C. Setliff*..........$2.95

Mid-Elementary

00412289 Andante Theme from "Surprise Symphony" (1P, 8H) / *Haydn, arr. Bilbro* $2.95

00406208 First Jazz (1P, 4H) / *Melody Bober*..........$2.50

00406789 Little Concertino in C (1P, 4H) / *Alexander Peskanov* $2.95

Later Elementary

00415178 Changing Places (1P, 4H) / *Edna Mae Burnam* $2.95

00406209 Puppy Pranks (1P, 4H) / *Melody Bober*..........$2.50

00416864 Rockin' Ragtime Boogie (1P, 4H) / *Glenda Austin*..........$3.99

00120780 Strollin' (1P, 4H) / *Carolyn Miller*..........$3.99

Early Intermediate

00416754 Bouquet (1P, 4H) / *Naoko Ikeda* $3.95

00113157 Dance in the City (1P, 4H) / *Naoko Ikeda* $3.99

00416843 Festive Celebration (1P, 4H) / *Carolyn Miller*..........$3.99

00114960 Fountain in the Rain (1P, 4H) / *William Gillock, arr. Austin*..........$3.99

00412287 Hungarian Dance No. 5 (1P, 4H) / *Brahms, arr. Wallis*..........$2.95

00416854 A Little Bit of Bach (1P, 4H) / *Glenda Austin* $3.99

00416921 Tango in D Minor (IP, 4H) / *Carolyn Miller*.......... $3.99

00416955 Tango Nuevo (1P, 4H) / *Eric Baumgartner* $3.99

Mid-Intermediate

00411831 Ave Maria (2P, 4H) / *Bach-Gounod, arr. Hinman*..........$2.95

00410726 Carmen Overture (1P, 6H) / *Bizet, arr. Sartorio*..........$3.95

00404388 Champagne Toccata (2P, 8H) / *William Gillock*.......... $3.99

00416762 Country Rag (2P, 4H) / *Alexander Peskanov* $4.95

00405212 Dance of the Sugar Plum Fairy / *Tchaikovsky, arr. Gillock* $3.99

00416959 Samba Sensation (1P, 4H) / *Glenda Austin*..........$3.99

00405657 Valse Elegante (1P, 4H) / *Glenda Austin*..........$3.95

Later Intermediate

00415223 Concerto Americana (2P, 4H) / *John Thompson* $5.95

00405552 España Cañi (1P, 4H) / *Marquina, arr. Gillock* $3.95

00405409 March of the Three Kings (1P, 4H) / *Bizet, arr. Gillock*..........$2.95

Advanced

00411832 Air (2P, 4H) / *Bach, arr. Hinman* $2.95

00405663 Habañera (1P, 4H) / *Stephen Griebling* $2.95

00405299 Jesu, Joy of Man's Desiring (1P, 4H) / *Bach, arr. Gillock*..........$3.95

00405648 Pavane (1P, 4H) / *Fauré, arr. Carroll*..........$2.95

View sample pages and hear audio excerpts online at **www.halleonard.com.**

www.willispianomusic.com

www.facebook.com/willispianomusic

Prices, contents, and availability subject to change without notice.

FOR MORE INFORMATION, SEE YOUR LOCAL MUSIC DEALER, OR WRITE TO:

HAL•LEONARD® CORPORATION

7777 W. BLUEMOUND RD. P.O. BOX 13819 MILWAUKEE, WI 53213